Twice as Weird: A Memoir about Being 2E

Peter Flom

February 22, 2024

Twice as Weird: A Memoir about Being 2E
[PUBLISHER, CITY ZIP]
©2024 by Peter Flom

All rights reserved. No part of this publication may be reproduced or distributed in any form or by any means, or stored in a database or retrieval system, without the prior written permission of the publisher, except by reviewers, who may quote brief passages in reviews.

Design by Indigo Editing and Publishing

ISBN: 979-8-218-37056-5.

Dedication

This book is for everyone who is 2E and all the people who love us.

Contents

Dedication i

Contents ii

Foreword v

Preface viii
    Me viii
    Weird ix
    On Truth x

1 Ledge   1

I Descent   4

2 Early   5

3 Five years old   8

4 Gateway   10

5 Eight years old   18

6 Nine and Ten   23

7 Tweens   38

CONTENTS

8 Early Teens	51
II Nadir	**60**
9 Ledge revisited	61
III Rise	**64**
10 Ages 15 and 16	65
11 Late teens	82
12 Not quite grown up	94
13 Israel	109
14 Adulthood at last	124
15 My 30s—Romance, more school, work	135
16 My early 40s—Could this be maturity?	165
17 My 50s and 60s	183
18 Now	196
IV Appendices	**200**
Appendices	201
Appendices	202
A Big school, small school, home school	203
B Stages of Acceptance	206
Stage 1: Denial	206
Stage 2: Depression	208

	Stage 3: Display 209	
	Stage 4: Dealing 210	

C Disability as a Mountain   **211**

D Nomenclature   **214**

E Mainstream   **216**

F Lazy   **218**

G Hey!   **220**

H Acknowledgements   **221**

Foreword

In the pages that follow, Peter Flom invites us into the rich and often misunderstood world of Twice Exceptional (2e) students through the lens of his own experiences. As we embark on this poignant journey, we find ourselves immersed in a narrative that goes beyond the conventional, urging us to reevaluate and recalibrate our understanding of learning differences and giftedness as well as our overall approach to education.

In the vast landscape of diverse learners, Twice Exceptional students stand out as individuals possessing extraordinary talents and unique challenges. Although 2e children are vastly different in a myriad of ways there are some similarities to note. So many 2e children are intensely eager to learn and become experts at various tasks and they often express incredibly intense emotions and struggle with dysregulation in ways that most typical children do not. As they grow into school-age children the distinctions between their gifts and areas of challenge become more apparent and, in many cases, the moments of dysregulation become more present and challenging, particularly in schools that do not have the experience and training to provide the needed academic, social emotional and executive functioning supports they require to thrive. Peter Flom's memoir serves as a testament to the importance of recognizing and embracing the needs of these exceptional minds within our education system. Too often, these students, who possess both exceptional abilities and learning differences, face a system that struggles to accommodate their dualities.

Peter's narrative underscores the urgency of acknowledging the nuanced needs of 2e students, who may excel in certain areas while grappling with challenges in others. It is a call to action for educators, parents, and policymakers to shift the paradigm and ensure that our education system is equipped to celebrate and leverage the strengths of 2e students. A common reason for the misinterpretation and subsequent ineffective responses to twice-exceptional (2e) children stems from the widespread assumption that being labeled as "gifted" implies inherent intelligence and talent, making academic tasks effortless. However, this oversimplification overlooks the complex nature of giftedness. In addition to intellectual abilities, characteristics such as a strong sense of perfectionism, and a delay in social-emotional maturity are often aspects of the gifted experience. It's crucial to recognize that having a learning difference alongside intellectual giftedness is not mutually exclusive; both can coexist within the 2e population.

Peter's story sheds light on the often-overlooked realm of twice exceptional (2e) education, highlighting the profound impact that personalized support and specialized training can have on these learners. Through his narrative, we see how an inclusive educational environment can cultivate a sense of belonging and understanding for 2e students, allowing them to thrive academically and socially. Furthermore, Peter's journey underscores the importance of recognizing and nurturing the unique talents and abilities of 2e individuals, rather than solely focusing on their challenges. By embracing a strengths-based approach, educators and policymakers can foster an atmosphere of acceptance and encouragement, enabling 2e learners to unleash their full potential and make meaningful contributions to their communities. Through his story, we are reminded of the imperative to advocate for greater awareness and resources for 2e education, ensuring that every student has the opportunity to thrive and succeed.

Peter's story is a beacon, guiding us towards a future where 2e students are no longer seen as challenging students, but instead are recognized for the unique and valuable perspectives they bring. It is a reminder that true educational equity requires a commitment to understanding and meeting the diverse needs of every learner.

In the end, this memoir is not just about one individual's journey; it is a collective narrative that calls on us to advocate for a more inclusive, responsive, and compassionate education system. Peter's lived experience as Twice Exceptional beckons us to create a world where every mind is valued, celebrated, and given the opportunity to flourish.

Preface

Me

Hi! I'm Peter and I'm twice exceptional. But until I was almost 40, that didn't exist.

I was born learning disabled, but the term "learning disabled" was born after me: It was first used in 1963, when I was four. Before that, a lot of neurodiverse people were said to have "minimal brain dysfunction," but that term was very rarely used. Really, the concept didn't exist before I was born.

And I'm also gifted. The combo is known as twice-exceptional, or 2E. But the term "2E" was only invented in the mid-1990s, when I was already in my 30's, and, according to Google Ngram viewer, it was very rare until the 21st century. I not only had to discover what I was, the world had to discover people like me could exist and come up with a name for us.

I'm a learning disabled adult. Yeah, yeah, a learning disabled adult. Not a "person with learning differences", I find that term kind of insulting. Everyone is different. I'm disabled. And, since "disabled" is defined a lot of ways, here's my definition:

> A disability is anything that disables you. That is, it makes it difficult or impossible to do something that most people do easily.

Disability is context specific in the sense that, in 15th century Europe, dyslexia was a very minor problem, because almost no one could read, anyway.

I get why people say "person with learning differences." They want to make us feel better. They want to emphasize the person. That's nice. But a) English puts adjectives before nouns. That's just how it works. We don't say "a person with shortness." And b) Minimizing someone's problem doesn't usually make them feel better. In fact, it makes them feel worse.

I'm a lot of other things too. I'm divorced. I'm the father of two adults. I've retired from a career as a statistician. I have written one book and many articles, both topical and academic. I've written poems and two of them are published (OK, published in very, very, niche places, but still). I have a PhD.

Weird

A lot of people who have helped me with this book have objected to the word "weird." I object to their objections. You lose stigma by claiming a condition, not by hiding it. I claim weird. "Weird" has a few different definitions. *The American Heritage Dictionary* defines it, in part, as:

> Strikingly odd or unusual, especially in an unsettling way.

and that is the sense in which I use it. I am unusual. And I unsettle people.

But just because I'm disabled doesn't mean I'm not able. In some areas, I am more than able, I am gifted. When I was in 5th grade I had a college level vocabulary (according to tests). I do math for fun.

It's not common to be learning disabled. It's a bit weird. We LD people are unusual and some of us unsettle some people. Maybe we shouldn't unsettle them, but we do. It's even weirder to have NLD rather than one of the better known LDs. It's not common to be gifted. It's a bit weird. And it's not at all common to be 2E. It's twice as weird.

On Truth

Nothing in this book is known by me to be false. The dialogue is nearly all invented, but I tried to capture the essence of what was said. I checked all the facts that I could, and corrected a bunch of memories that were wrong.

Chapter 1

Ledge

It's around 10 PM on a fall evening in 1973. I am 14 years old and I am sitting on the ledge of the window of my room on the eighth floor of 31 East 79th Street in Manhattan, thinking about falling. Not jumping, since I am too scared to stand on the ledge. My brother, Jason, is across the hall in his room, unaware. I don't know if he's asleep yet, or still practicing on his electric guitar with no amp. My parents are downstairs, blissfully unaware, maybe they are asleep already. My sister, Nancy, is in Chicago with her husband, unaware that I am sitting on a ledge, but somewhat aware of her favorite brother's problems, because we talk about them a lot. I talk to her, rather than our mother, because Nancy listens without judging, while Mom judges without listening.

It's a cool night, but I do not go downstairs to get my coat, as my mother would doubtless wonder why I'm taking my winter coat upstairs. I shiver a bit, with even my skinny tush not quite supported by the ledge.

I wonder: If I don't manage to fall on my head, will I die? I've not yet learned to dive into water, will I figure a way to invert and fall on my head? That would surely kill me. Or will I screw this up too? It would suck to break my legs and hips and be in the hospital in pain with my parents and everyone wondering what the hell is wrong with me, despite everything.

I wonder where I would fall. What's down there? It's not the street. I can't really see what is down there exactly, I'd have to lean way out and look down and I've never done that. I can't picture where it is, relative to streets and avenues. Is it an alley? I don't know. Would anyone find me before my mother makes breakfast in the morning and wonders where I am, and calls. And calls. And then climbs the stairs to find the window wide open and no Peter.

I think some more and, after a few minutes, I realize that, if I succeed in killing myself, I won't ever be able to undo it. It seems like it would be wonderful to not be, but what if it isn't? I can't undo it. Death is final. On the other hand, I can always kill myself tomorrow. If I decide one way, it's forever. If I decide the other, it's still open. I read Hamlet earlier that year and Hamlet puts it well:

> To be, or not to be, that is the question:
> Whether 'tis nobler in the mind to suffer
> The slings and arrows of outrageous fortune,
> Or to take arms against a sea of troubles
> And by opposing end them.
>
> And thus the native hue of resolution
> Is sicklied o'er with the pale cast of thought,
> And enterprises of great pith and moment
> With this regard their currents turn awry And lose the
>   name of action.

Queen puts it well as well:

> Mama! I don't want to die. I sometimes wish I'd never been born at all.

So, I get back into my room somehow; glad I managed not to fall by accident after deciding not to fall on purpose. I close the window against the chill, lie down on the floor with its nice warm rug, get some paper, and write this:

Have you ever?

> Have you ever been out on a ledge, looking down?
> Have you ever felt fear and hate all around?
> Have you ever seen warfare inside your own soul?
> Have you ever known that you'd *never* be whole?

> And yet for some reason you crawl on back in
> Like Hamlet from Shakespeare, but which is the sin?
> To jump, fall and die, and thus to be free
> Or to be a coward, like Hamlet and me?

I stand up and get into bed. But I keep thinking. I'm not depressed. Other than almost killing myself and not sleeping very well, I have no symptoms of depression. I'm not sad. I'm not uninterested. It isn't hard to get up in the morning. There are things I like to do, like math and chess and reading and eating. I love my sister and brother. It's just that death is so much easier than life.

Then I go to sleep. In the morning, my mother makes breakfast for her two sons. And I don't tell anyone, not even my therapist Dr. Weintrob; not even Nancy.

Part I

Descent

Chapter 2

Early

I am 0 years old. Or even less. I've just been born. I was due a bit before Labor Day but I came out before the 4th of July, 1959. Seven months after my parents' wedding. I was seven weeks early. At least, that's what they've always said.

I am weird. Although I am very early, I am not so small: A little over 5 pounds (2.3 kg). But I have no nails on my fingers or toes, and no sucking reflex. For a while, I have to be fed with something like an eye dropper. I know, because my mother told me.

Like other newborns, my eyes don't focus well, but even after my left eye learns to focus, my right doesn't; it wanders. It wanders so much that sometimes when people look at me they only see the white. But I start walking and babbling and talking at the normal times, although, for a long while, I am hard to understand. At first, this is because I don't enunciate very clearly; later on, it is because I read a lot and guess at how words are pronounced.

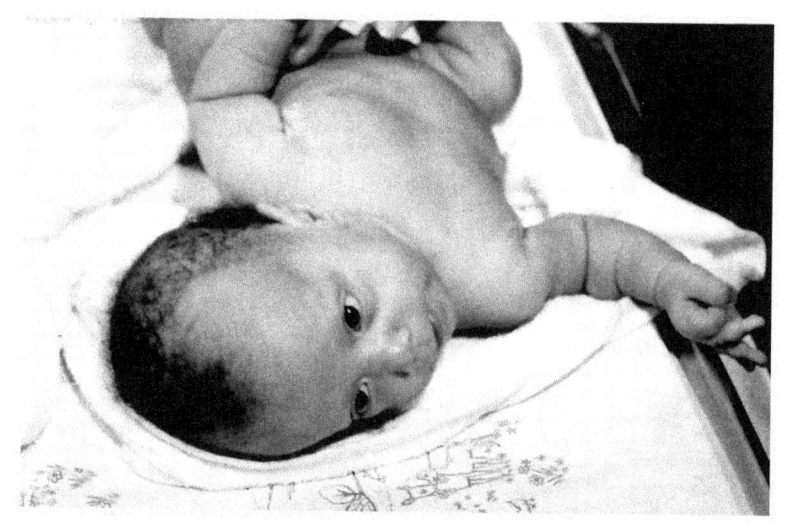

Birth

There are three grownups around. Mommy, of course. And Nancy, who is also a grownup at 12, and sometimes Daddy. Nancy really likes me. Nancy thinks I'm cute. And, after 20 months, there's my baby brother, Jason. He has big pudgy cheeks and red hair and blue eyes. Everyone thinks he's cute.

When Jason first starts to babble, I understand him before Mom does, and I translate for him, telling her what he wants, like a bottle or a diaper change.

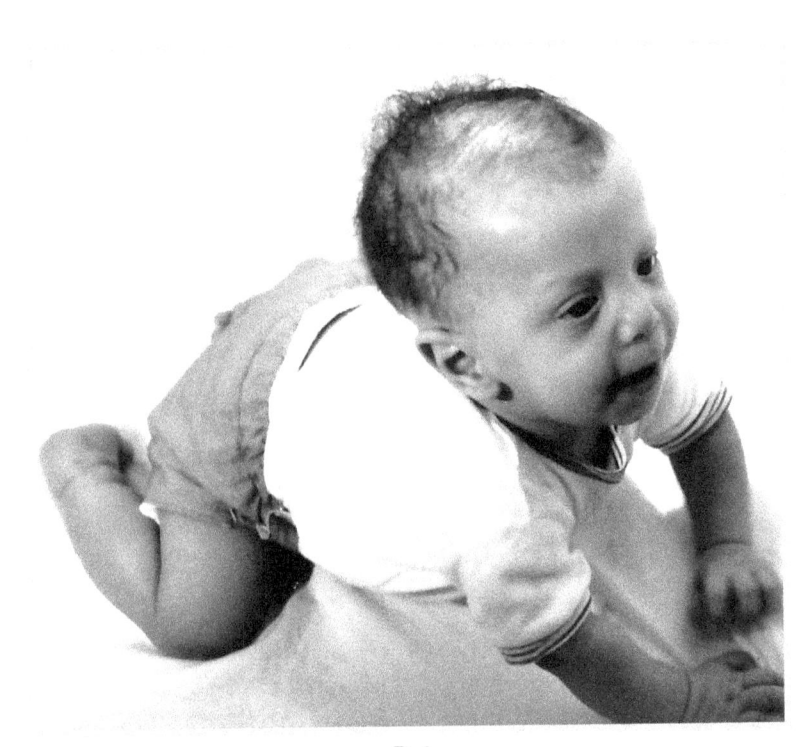

Baby

Chapter 3

Five years old

I am five years old and in kindergarten at the Rudolf Steiner School in New York. Nancy went there and liked it, so I guess it was a sort of default choice. Things aren't going well. The kids are doing things and I'm doing them wrong. They clap to songs and I clap wrong. They take naps and I jump on my cot. Who needs sleep? All the other kids can cut things and color things and I can't figure out scissors and crayons. I always pick the scissors up wrong. I don't hold the crayon right, and I can't make it do what I want. I know what I'm drawing is wrong, but I can't make it right. I try to sing and my voice comes out wrong, even worse than the other kids, and I can't fix that, either.

There is clearly something wrong with me. No one tells me there is something wrong, but I know. All those kids do all those things better than I do. But what is wrong?

I don't know how I knew something was wrong. But I know. And that doesn't feel good.

But some things are right with me.

Friends of my parents have just had a baby. Her name is Sabha and her mom is Rosalinda. Sabha looks like a baby. She has chubby cheeks and dark brown hair. I hear some people say she looks like Winston Churchill; I don't know who that is, so I figure he looks like Sabha. He must be cute because Sabha is.

Rosalinda also has dark hair. She's shorter than Mommy, and heavier. I don't know where Sabha's daddy is.

> *I later found out that he had died right around the time of her birth. He was much older than his wife (he was born in 1902, so he was 20 years older than my dad) but still too young to die, and had been my dad's mentor, which is how they became friends of ours.*

Rosalinda and Sabha come to our house a lot, several times a week. Sabha is like my little sister; Jason is, in some ways, more like my twin, even though he's 20 months younger.

One day, Rosalinda and Sabha and my parents and my brother and I are all in a car together, traveling to their summer house. Daddy is driving and Rosalinda and Mommy are in the front seat. Sabha and Jason and I are sharing the back seat.

Rosalinda and my parents are discussing child rearing. Rosalinda says "I will spank Sabha so she learns self-discipline." "No, Wasawinda," I chime in from the back seat, "that won't teach *self*-discipline but *other*-discipline. And, it will teach Sabha that might makes right, and that strong people could force weaker people to do things."

"You're right." Rosalinda replies.

Me at age 5

Chapter 4

Gateway

I am five years old (or maybe just turned six). It's summer and we are staying in a house.

I am sitting on porch in our backyard with six kids I don't know and one adult, Mrs. Freidus, a gray haired lady, also sitting on the porch. All our parents are standing around watching. Mrs. Freidus is talking to us kids. And listening to us.

Elizabeth Freidus teaching us. I am in red.

Mrs. Freidus holds up an apple and asks: "How many pieces do I need to cut so we can each have one?" There is discussion, which settles on seven or eight. And I say "Well, it could be either, because there are seven kids and eight people." Mrs. Freidus turns to my mother and says "Oy! A Yeshiva bucher."[1]

---

[1] "Yeshiva bucher" in Yiddish is, literally, a student in a yeshiva, but it also means a hair-splitter.

> *I later found out that, as a young woman, Elizabeth (Mrs. Freidus) had had a stroke or something and one side of her face was paralyzed. Doctor after doctor had said there was nothing to be done, sorry. But she persisted and found one who said that* maybe *if she stared at her face in a mirror for hours and concentrated on that part of her face, day after day, she* might *have some improvement. She did that. Her face looked normal when I knew her, except that, when she was very tired, one eye sort of drooped a bit, but I didn't notice that when I was a kid.*

Now I am six. I'm in a new school, it's called Gateway. It's weird! It's inside another building. And it's got a great big gym but only one classroom. And an office where Mommy sits with Mrs. Freidus.

There are only three students! David and Cordelia and me. David is a nice boy, with yellow hair and glasses. Cordelia is big! Our teacher is Grace Kumar, who has hair even longer than Nancy's! It goes down past her tushy! When we are rough with each other, she says "be gentle, that's a person you're playing with."

It's going well. Mrs. Kumar is really nice, and she works with each of us on whatever we are bad at (I am bad at handwriting and drawing and taking turns and dressing neatly and so on). Later that year, two more kids join us, Todd and Keith. And we get another room.

> *Many years later, I found out that Rudolf Steiner had asked me not to return. My parents took me to a psychologist who told them I had "minimal brain dysfunction" and "would never go to college." Mom responded by finding out all she could about kids like me, which led her to Elizabeth, and, together, they started Gateway. My mom did everything that wasn't education and Elizabeth did everything that was.*

***

Now I'm seven and the school is growing, and still going well. But, no matter how many people try to teach me how to hold a pencil, I can't do it right. And no matter who tries to teach me to draw, it doesn't work. At all. So I can't print or write anything remotely legible and I can't draw at all, I can't make a pen or pencil do what I want. Other kids' drawings are much better than mine. But it's not such a big deal here.

And I can't remember where things are. When I put something down, or away, it's gone. Other kids seem to just know, somehow, where things are. But it's different here, not like Rudolph Steiner. It's softer. Mrs. Kumar and Miss Monroe and Miss Pulanco never get angry or impatient and they cope better with my frustration. The other kids don't care that I don't do what they do.

> *Over the years, at least six or seven people tried to teach me how to hold a pencil and more than a dozen tried to teach me to draw. And people say things like "everyone can draw." No. Not everyone can. The attempted teaching is frustrating. The attitude even more so.*

One time, they put a blindfold on kids and ask them to find their way across the room. Some kids do it great, they walk to the right spot with no stopping or gaps. Others get confused, and can't exactly find their way without help. When they put the blindfold on me I start screaming! Everything is GONE! I can't find my way across the room, the room is gone. And I scream some more and they take the mask away. I go in the kitchen with one teacher to calm down. But no one makes me feel different or bad or weird or whatever; unlike what happened at Steiner and unlike what happens at home. It's not that other people actively *try* to make me feel bad, they just do it. But at Gateway, they figure out how not to.

***

SternBlocks

Mrs. Stern teaches us math using Stern blocks.

The other kids are so slow! They are just using them to count, or add, or even just compare sizes. Seven is bigger than four. But I'm thinking. How can I use them to multiply? Hmmm. I can't make them into a rectangle, there aren't enough blocks. I can't stack them ... I think and think and then I figure it out! I have the solution! It's so *cool*. I yell out. I don't raise my hand. I need to tell Mrs. Stern! She needs to know.

PETER: Mrs. Stern! Look! If you do this and this and this, you can get 4 times 3!
MRS. STERN: I never thought of that! Show me again. I didn't know you could do that, and I invented these things!

Teaching the teacher (the inventor!) feels good. But figuring it out feels good all by itself.

Mommy sits in the office with Mrs. Freidus, but she doesn't really talk to us kids during the day. I don't know what she does. But I find out she and Mrs. Freidus started the school for me! That's cool. But I start to wonder why I need a whole school just for me. And why do the other kids need it?

***

My brother Jason and I are so different. Not only do we look very different, and go to different schools (he stayed at Steiner for five years), we act different in all sorts of ways. Even how we sleep. Jason sleeps on his back and likes to be tucked in very tight. In the morning, he slides out and the bed looks like it was just made. I sleep on my stomach and, in the morning, the pillow is on the floor, the sheets are tangled around me, and the blanket could be anywhere.

Jason, like our dad, falls asleep as soon as his head touches the pillow, I toss around. And about once a month I don't sleep at all and just stay up all night, reading and thinking and worrying about school or friends or the state of the world or almost anything.

Jason is making friends, playing sports, doing normal kid things. I'm not.

Jason and I are not competitive with each other. We cooperate. Although he is 20 months younger than I am, we are more like twins, because I am behind on things and he isn't. We play games, some of which we invent ourselves. We play Crossfire, which has a big flat board and a little rolly thing, and each of us has a little gun that shoots tiny steel balls with which we try to move the thing. We play garage, where we build a garage out of blocks and have cars go in and park and then leave and I make up a price list. We play with Hot Wheels. It's fun. We always manage to either have competition without getting too intense, or to pool our talents to make up a game.

> *Years later, I find out about sibling rivalry and so on. I'm surprised that this seems to be almost universal, as Jason and I didn't ever have that.*

***

In our apartment Jason and I share a bedroom and Nancy has a tiny room behind the kitchen. I go in there a lot to talk to her, either before or after dinner, or on weekends, or whenever she is around. I sit on her bed or a chair, we listen to music (a lot of Peter, Paul, and Mary, and other folk music). We talk about everything. We agree that the war in Vietnam is stupid and that civil rights are good. She's so much nicer than Mom. She actually seems to want to talk to me, and to talk about me, and to listen to me. Mom only wants to talk about what she wants to talk about, and doesn't seem to listen to me whenever I talk about anything good.

Nancy has very long hair, way down her back. I'm amazed by how long it takes her to wash and dry her hair. My hair is dry a few minutes after I wash it.

I meet some of her friends and boyfriends, all of whom are nice to me. A lot of them are political, some of her boyfriends are draft-dodgers (this was the middle of the Vietnam War) and I am already pretty political myself. They seem to welcome this odd little kid into their conversations; at least, it feels like that. But her room is so small that there's not much room for groups of friends, usually one or two at most.

> *Looking back, I am sure they did a lot of things on their own and I'm less sure how they felt about me. Maybe they resented my presence but Nancy took my side. And Nancy was surely doing a lot of things without me, but it didn't feel like it at the time. She was in her late teens. She had school and all sorts of outside life. But that life was so hidden from me that it almost didn't exist; sort of the way that little kids don't realize that their teachers have lives outside of school.*

Chapter 5

Eight years old

I am eight years old and I am home from school, sick. I'm lying on the couch in our living room. I don't remember the couch. I don't remember the living room. Probably on the advice of some bookseller or maybe a teacher, Mommy has gotten me *A Wrinkle in Time* by Madeleine L'Engle. I open the book and begin.

> It was a dark and stormy night.
>
> In her attic bedroom Margaret Murry, wrapped in an old patchwork quilt, sat on the foot of the bed and watched the trees tossing in the frenzied lashing of the wind. Behind the trees clouds scudded frantically across the sky. Every few moments the moon ripped through them, creating wraithlike shadows that raced along the ground.
>
> The house shook.
>
> Wrapped in her quilt, Meg shook.
>
> She wasn't usually afraid of the weather.—It's not just the weather, she thought.—It's the weather on top of everything else. On top of me. On top of Meg Murry doing everything wrong.

I am hooked, like a fish. Not by the scene of Meg in her attic—I live in a New York City apartment and know little of shaking homes or windy attics—but by the "everything else". By the "On top of me", by the "doing everything wrong". It's not so much any particular thing; it's a feeling of being wrong, of being broken, of being weird.

I read that book from cover to cover. Then I start over. I am Meg, despite being years younger and a boy; I'm her, with her brilliant parents. I'm her little brother Charles Wallace too, the extra-odd member of that odd family. I wish I was her twin brothers, who are normal, like Jason.

Before this, I knew how to read, but now I am a reader.

I borrow books from Nancy, who is studying literature at Chatham College; some of them are college texts on mythology, but she loans me any books that she thinks her weird, precocious, troubled little brother will like. I borrow books from the school library and the public library (and read them in class). I buy books at bookstores. And I even steal a book (the only time I break the law, but ... I need that book!)

A Wrinkle in Time also turns me into a lover of science fiction, even though it is fantasy. I become Thorby and Balsim from *Citizen of the Galaxy* and Valentine Michael Smith from *Stranger in a Strange Land* and Susan Calvin from Isaac Asimov's robot novels and more and more. I go places. I rendezvous with Rama. When I'm them, there, I can stop being me, here. It might be scary or interesting or funny or anything. But I can always leave: Just close the book.

One thing that happens when you read is that you learn things. And one thing I learn is that other people see things in their heads a lot more than I do. They can picture themselves in different places; places they've been and even places they haven't been. I don't do this. I learn that people look certain ways, that their faces express emotions that I don't recognize. I know they do because writers write things like "he had a quizzical expression" and, while I know what each word means, I have no idea what a quizzical expression is.

***

Rosalinda and Sabha come to our apartment a lot, but in the summers, we sometimes visit them in Rockport, Massachusetts. Sabha and I play together a lot, more than she does with Jason. I already like little kids a lot. Jason, being a more typical kid of six, doesn't really want to play with a three year old baby, but I do.

On this trip, we are sitting outside on the lawn. Sabha and I are a little apart from the grownups and I say "Sabha, when we get big, will you marry me?" She accepts, which I knew she would, but she is only three and doesn't understand it the way a big boy like me does! I have figured it out. I'm a boy, she's a girl, we love each other, so ... marriage! Also, it's OK that I'm older because Daddy is older than Mommy.

I am weird but reading is fun and Sabha said "yes".

Sabha and me, around the time that I proposed

***

I'm lying in bed wondering how I can compete with my father. I don't know why I'm wondering this, it just seems to be what you're supposed to do. I figure I started way ahead of him, and that, therefore, to be fair, I can only win by winding up way ahead of him. He started poor, I did not. His parents were immigrants who had little formal schooling, mine were born here and had lots of schooling. I own lots of books. I have all sorts of things he didn't have. And he went to Harvard Law and became a very successful lawyer.

How can I possibly win? What would I have to be? President, maybe. Or a Supreme Court Justice. I don't think I can do that, so I decide not to compete professionally. But maybe I can be a better father, so I set that as a goal.

Chapter 6

Nine and Ten

I am nine years old and I am a mess. Nancy has gone off to college, so I have no one to talk to and my parents and Jason and I all rub harder against each other. Some nights, Jason hides under the dining table during dinner, I think to avoid all the arguing and conflict. I don't know what's wrong with me. At school I am more or less OK, but outside of school I am angry a lot. No one else knows what's wrong with me, either. Most people act like I am lazy, crazy, or stupid, even my parents do. I get angry at my parents. I give them the silent treatment for days at a time, not speaking to them at all.

I figure out that the bathroom is one place where I can be alone (it's just Jason and me sharing a bathroom, so there is never a problem with several people using it). So I take long baths.

And even Gateway can't really handle me. I'm bored at school. I learn the stuff faster than the other kids. They decide I need a mainstream school.

My parents know something is wrong but do not know what. Maybe they are worried about my transition to a mainstream school where there would be much less support. They decide I need a therapist.

> *I think that, at this point, my mother knew I was "learning disabled." That term began to be used around the time Gateway got started, and I believe Elizbeth Freidus used it. But, then, why am I so good at learning? What I really am is 2E, or twice exceptional, but that term didn't start getting used until around 1990, when I was well into adulthood. And it wasn't just a new term, it was a new idea—that you could be both LD and gifted.*

Mom and I go to 12 West 96th Street, the office of Dr. Alex Weintrob. Mom calls him a "worry doctor". I'm a little nervous, but not too much. While we are sitting there, waiting, the kid who comes before me leaves and shouts back to him "See you next time, Winey!" which strikes me as odd but liberating. I always call adults by their title and their last name. If a kid can call an adult "Winey" then almost everything must be allowed in his office.

His office has three rooms. There's a waiting room that he shares with someone else (I see a white door with a nameplate). There's a painting on the wall. Three blobs of color and a signature: "Miro". I think this is stupid. And Miro's signature is even worse than mine! It's just four big letters, not even really printed.

He comes out to greet us. He's got dark brown hair and glasses with yellow rims. He's wearing a jacket and tie. He shows me the other two rooms, one has comfortable chairs and a couch and a lot of empty space and art on the walls and carpet and stuff. The other has bare floors, small chairs, a formica table, and lots of toys and dolls. We go in that room, which I can tell is for kids.

After we sit in the little chairs, Dr. Weintrob tells me that everything I say will be confidential. I nod, but I also know that not all people are trustworthy, especially my mom.

For a few years, I've been sure that I'm allergic to fish. But my symptoms are all internal—whenever I eat fish, I get a weird feeling like a rash on the inside of my mouth. I tell my mother but she is sure I am not allergic. We argue about it. She's convinced she is right, so she serves us fish for dinner and tells us it isn't fish. Of course, it's pretty obvious that it's fish. I still feel ill after eating fish (even if Mom has told me it isn't fish), but I now know not to trust my mom.

I want to tell Dr. Weintrob things about my mother. Bad things. That she doesn't love me or know how to help me. Tell him that she would also betray confidences, not by telling secrets to other people, but by using things I said to her as tools for fighting with me later on. And I want to tell him bad things about myself. That I am suicidal and angry and lonely. And I want to tell him I'm smart, which seems bad to tell someone. But I don't want these things to get back to Mom.

I decide I have to test him. I think about good ways to do it. At our next session I calmly say

"I am going to kill my parents."

Even before I tell him, I wonder what will happen. Will the police show up? I picture a couple of cops in uniform ringing our doorbell. Will my parents get furious?

"How do you plan to do it?" he asks, equally calmly.

But I just say "I don't know". I haven't thought that out. I haven't actually planned on killing them, just on testing Dr. Weintrob. We move on.

Nothing happens. Not when Mom and I get home. Not later that day, not all week. No cops. No fury. He didn't tell. I can trust him.

That done, it is great to have our weekly appointments. He's a sort of substitute for Nancy. He likes me regardless of what I say (even that I'm going to kill my parents). He pays attention to me, whatever I am doing. And I can say anything. Each week, I see him on Thursday afternoon after school. So Fridays are good, and the weekends are OK, but Wednesdays and Thursdays are not good at all. I feel tensions growing until I see him. My temper gets shorter, I sleep worse, I fight more, I get more stomach aches. And when he goes on vacation, things get much worse at home and school. I don't know what it is, but I gradually figure it out. That weekly hour is a grace period.

At one point, fairly early on, Dr. Weintrob says, "Your mother has been calling me to find out what you are saying in here, but I haven't told her." That's typical, I think. Of course she wants to spy on me. But the fact that Dr. Weintrob tells me is great. It reinforces my trust. After all, he didn't need to say anything, and, if he was telling her things, he would hardly tell me she was asking.

We play a lot of checkers while we talk, but I move to the grownup room pretty fast. I don't want to play with dolls and I certainly don't want to draw or paint and checkers is OK but, really, I like to talk. He asks me if I'd prefer the other room and I say I would.

At his recommendation, my parents send me for another neuropsychological battery of tests. Dr. Weintrob recommends Dr. Wolf. I look forward to it. I like tests! I read books of puzzles for fun. I start reading Martin Gardner's books of puzzles starting around this age, and there's a big book called something like *539 Mathematical Puzzles*. I like knowing how I think and figuring out more about me.

On the day of the test, Mom takes me to Dr. Wolf's office on Fifth Avenue. I spend most of the day with him. I know I'm being tested and I know that it will take a while. As the day goes on, I know I'm doing well on some tests and badly on others, and that some were not the sort where you do well or badly. Neither Dr. Wolf or Dr. Weintrob tell me that, it's just obvious. Some are for ability and some are not.

One ability test is the WISC, which is an IQ test. It has subtests. One subtest is a bunch of questions that are just information about things. Most of them are so easy!

But one is "where does the sun rise?" This ought to be easy, but I can not remember, despite living in Manhattan, where the streets line up with east and west, and despite walking into the sun rising or setting every day on the way to or from school. I know it's east or west and I try to figure it out from knowing that the usual direction of weather flow was west-to-east, and from the fact that it's earlier in Chicago than New York. But I don't manage that. I'm so stupid! It's so annoying!

I do know that it depends on your latitude and on the season. The right answer isn't "east" or "west" but much more complicated. It's winter now, so it's either southeast or southwest. I know he wants either "east" or "west", but I can't figure it out and I don't remember. I guess "west".

Dr. Wolf keeps asking questions and they are gradually getting harder. I know that the "east west" question was too easy for me to miss at age nine. But, as they get harder, I keep getting them right and I can sort of tell that I'm getting some right that most nine year old kids couldn't answer.

I'm not sure how I could tell, I think I just knew that these are things I had learned in ways that most kids my age didn't.

That feels good. But I keep wondering not so much why I am smart or knowledgeable, but why other kids are stupid and ignorant.

Now he gives me blocks. Each side of each cube is either solid red, solid white, or half red and half white, on a diagonal.

He gives me patterns to copy. The first ones are 2x2 and I manage those. But then he gives me 3x3 patterns I can't do anything. I sort of randomly scramble the blocks, but that doesn't work. I'm simply staring at the cubes and don't even know how to start. I know I'm doing really badly. I'm thinking that they wouldn't give kids a task that was impossible, but it is impossible for me. I just stare at the blocks, feeling like an idiot. Weird. Why am I so stupid?

Now he gives me little tiles with cartoon characters on them doing things. I am supposed to put them into a logical order, but, without any words on the tiles, they make no sense to me. I'm just randomly shuffling the tiles, or staring at them without moving them. I'm so frustrated! I don't know how badly I'm messing up. The number of tiles increases, and they are timed. I don't know if I'm supposed to get them all, or how fast I'm supposed to do so. I'm mad at myself for being stupid and I'm frustrated because I don't know how stupid I am being. And I really need to know!

Finally that subtest is over and now there are arithmetic questions. I get them all. And I wonder how other kids can miss such easy questions. But some kids must, or the test wouldn't be designed this way. They wouldn't ask only easy questions. These questions are kind of boring, but kind of fun. And getting all the answers feels good. How can I be so smart *and* so stupid?

> *Even then, my brain worked this way. I knew some of the questions would have to be easy and some hard for the scoring to work. I don't know how I knew that, I just did.*

On one test, Dr. Wolf asks me to fill in the blank after various phrases. I fill in a few phrases with no big reactions from Dr. Wolf. Then he says "I am ..." and I say "reasonably intelligent" and he says "you're underestimating yourself." That feels good.

When I leave his Fifth Avenue office that afternoon, I see the sun setting over Central Park. In the west. It rises in the east. I got it wrong. Why am I so stupid? I am immediately determined not to get this wrong EVER AGAIN, so I make up a mnemonic. "Sets" almost rhymes with "west" so, I will know, forever, where the sun rises.

I'm at my next session with Dr. Weintrob, going over the results. I'm very eager and curious to see my scores. Dr. Wolf's report is pretty long and we go over it slowly. Usually, in our sessions, we sit facing each other, but for this, we sit side by side. He is confused about my scores on the IQ test. He expresses amazement at how well I did on some things and how poorly on others. On one subtest I got the equivalent of 60 and on another, the equivalent of 160. He tells me that people don't get the pattern of scores I got.

And then there were the other tests, that are supposed to say other things about me. I enjoy reviewing them. I'm interested in me and how I work and don't work and what is going on in my head. And I also like tests in the abstract. I would like going over someone else's tests almost as much as going over mine.

Overall, I'm very glad to have taken the WISC. While I was taking it, I got a bit frustrated, but, as soon as I go over it with Dr. Weintrob it became solid evidence that I am not lazy, crazy, or stupid, which are all things I was called. I'm "learning disabled" Dr. Weintrob tells me. And we talk about that a bit. I'm still weird, and my LD doesn't fit what LD are supposed to be, but it's better than lazy, crazy, or stupid.

> *While I was at Gateway, learning disabilities got invented and started becoming known, a little. And either Dr. Wolf or Dr. Weintrob can use the phrase. I don't know if Dr. Wolf wrote it and Dr. Weintrob just read it or not; probably Dr. Wolf wrote it, as it was still a pretty rare term. But, while LD has started to become known, NVLD has not.*

***

One night, lying in bed before falling asleep, I figure something out. There's something wrong with Mom. I don't know what it is, but something isn't right. And I also figure out that a lot of what she says is nonsense. But even though I figure this out, I still listen. She's my mother, after all. And I'm only 9, so, even though I've figured out that she's wrong a lot, my heart isn't always listening to my brain.

Some time after this, Dr. Weintrob tells me that he had called my mom to recommend that she and Dad and Jason all come in together, but that Mom refused to consider it, although Dad was willing. After all my talk about Mom and Dad and Jason, I'm not really surprised he wanted to talk to them too, and I'm not surprised that Mom refused. *She* doesn't need therapy and the reasons *I* do can't possibly have anything to do with her! I know that's how she feels and I want to be there when Dr. Weintrob tells her she is wrong and that she is messing up motherhood.

***

It's spring and I just started in a new school—Emerson. It's at 12 East 96th Street and I notice it's exactly opposite Dr. Weintrob's office, which is 12 *West* 96th Street. It's much bigger than Gateway. I'm entering in the middle of 4th grade. I'm not really sure why. I'm shorter than most of the class, and very skinny, and my hair is cut short but you can still tell that it's very dark and very curly.

My teacher is Mrs. Caushen. She is nice, but her usual punishment of kids is to make us go sit in the kindergarten class. That's not punishment, that's reward! She also often tells us we are "too old to be cute."

There's a girl who lines up a little ahead of me each morning. She's an older woman—a 6th grader—named Cecilia. And the Simon and Garfunkel song Cecilia is on the radio a lot. Oof!. I'm not quite clear on what "making love in the afternoon, with Cecilia, up in my bedroom" means, but I am sure I want to do it. Mostly, I see Cecilia from behind, so I'm more sure that she has long, medium brown hair, than what her face looks like. But, unlike most of the girls in elementary school she is shaped like a girl. I am delighted by that.

Things are not going so well at Emerson. At Gateway, I had been accepted by other kids and even celebrated by some teachers. I hadn't felt weird. I mean, I knew I was odd for liking math and being good at it, but, at Gateway, odd was OK. We were all odd. And the tininess of the school meant that everyone was supervised all the time. But now?

Other kids are again doing things I don't understand, or even recognize, even when I (in a poor way) do them. They are making friends, which I do a little. They are forming groups, which I don't do, at all. I see and hear the same kids talking to each other consistently. They eat lunch together. We all eat at big communal tables, but I mostly just sit by myself and eat and read.

I do make three friends, somehow. I don't know how. Peter Neski, Adam Redfield, and Steven Mack. Steven is a nice kid, but his family and mine are very different. For one thing, when I go to Steve's house, they watch news on TV during dinner! There isn't a TV in our dining room or living room or kitchen.

In addition to prohibiting TV at dinner, Mom has a long list of topics that are "not dinner table conversation". I can talk about just about anything over a meal, but I can understand that there are things a lot of people don't like talking about while eating (like, say, bodily functions, or decaying bodies). But my mother's list seems to include any topic she doesn't like or doesn't know a lot about, like, say, math. I'll say something like "in math we learned about factoring..." and she'll say "that's not dinner table conversation" and then bring up some other topic. This happens more than once! Math is fascinating stuff! Luckily, I am interested in the other things they talk about also; I'm interested in a lot of things!

One Saturday night, Steven sleeps over at our house. When we wake up, we got to the kitchen and Steven says "Let's make pancakes!" I say "How do you make pancakes?" "It's easy! Where's your Bisquick?" and I say "What's Bisquick?" And he just looks at me. So we had cereal.

Mom makes pancakes sometimes, but always from scratch.

At Emerson, other kids mostly ignore me, mostly a sort of shunning. I'm not sure what is going on. When I get called "weirdo" or "retard" I remember the scores I got on the WISC, and I remind myself that I am not lazy, crazy, or stupid. But I am learning disabled.

As a defense against the shunning and dislike, I decide to be obnoxious on purpose. Sometimes I pick my nose and leave it on my finger. Now, when other kids don't like me, it's not really me. Except, yes, really.

I read all the time. I read while walking down the street, I read in the bath, when I'm sitting in the lunchroom, I read, I read while waiting for food, I read while eating. Usually I read books but one day, when I'm eating lunch by myself, I read the milk container:

> The contents of this container is not fit for human consumption.

That's funny! Don't drink the milk! Of course they *meant* the container itself. But why didn't they say that? Grownups are stupid.

In 5th grade my class takes the Stanford Achievement Test. We spend a couple hours filling in bubbles that relate to English and math and other subjects. It's really easy. It's kind of fun, but it's kind of boring because it's easy. But it feels good to know I am doing well.

Some time later we get our scores back on a printed form with a score for each test and lines in between and stanine scores (which they explain) and grade equivalents. I do well on all of them. But on reading comprehension, my score is *above* 12th grade. The chart for converting "number correct" into "grade level" only went to a certain limit. I got beyond that. I broke the test! I hear teachers talk about me to each other with some wonder. I wonder why they have scores that can't be scaled properly. But it feels good to do so well.

Weird. But good weird. Now I have more evidence against being lazy, crazy, or stupid. Well, at least against "stupid."

***

My math teacher is Mrs. Finn. She is old and stupid! She keeps giving us work sheets with lots of arithmetic problems. Two digits times two digits. I get them wrong. Who wants to memorize times tables? I like math, not arithmetic! And, even when I do get the right answer, she marks some of them wrong because my handwriting is so messy. Still, no one has managed to teach me to write neatly, none of the methods I try work. I can't even hold a pen a good way, even if I look at diagrams or people show me. It's really frustrating!

But I like math.

On TV I see an ad for Clorox Bleach that says something like "Clorox gets clothes 42% cleaner than clothes washed without Clorox." I wonder how you measure cleanliness in percent? Do they add up the dirt molecules? Do they take a poll? How do they find out? And why don't they tell us in the ad? It's so annoying! Why don't people complain about this? The ad makes no sense!

Another ad is for Trident gum. It says "4 out of 5 dentists surveyed recommend sugarless gum for their patients who chew gum." And I think: So, 1 out of 5 recommend gum with sugar? That seems high. If sugar is so bad for your teeth, why would even 20% of dentists recommend it?

And why only dentists who were surveyed? Did they run multiple surveys and just take the best one? Did they only survey dentists they liked? Why don't other people think this way? Why don't they suspect that the whole thing is bogus, or that they are being lied to?

At dinner, I bring up interesting math questions but Mom says that this is not dinner table conversation. I figure this is probably because math is not her strong subject.

Stupid Mrs. Finn tells my parents that I need remedial math over the summer. It's funny! I'm probably the best in math in the whole school! That's what the standardized tests say. And even I can manage to fill in bubbles so they can be read. Mrs. Finn is an idiot.

***

Now it's summer and, thanks to Mrs. Finn, a woman is coming to teach me math, all by myself! It's wonderful!

> *I don't remember what she looked like at all; I couldn't say if she was Black or white, tall or short, or anything. I also don't remember what she sounded like. But the math was fun.*

We do exponents. We do logarithms. We do some algebra. I learn some tricks for times tables. And I make some up myself.

- Two times is just double. Double 3 and you get 6. No problem.

- Ten times is just add a 0. Add a 0 to 5 and get 50. $5*10 = 50$.

- Three times is double plus the starting number. $5*3$ is double 5 plus 5 is 15.

- Four times is double double. $6*4$ is double six for 12 and double 12 for 24.

- Five times is easy to remember, it's an easy pattern, but I make up a trick anyway: Divide by two. If it comes out even, add a zero. If it comes out with a remainder, add a 5. 7x5. Divide 7 by 2 it's 3 and a remainder, so add a 5 to the 3 to get 35.

- There are *lots* of tricks for nine times. I learn the finger trick: Hold out your hand, palms facing away, fingers pointed up. Now, your left pinky is 1 and your left ring finger is 2 and so on, to your right pinky which is 10. If you want to multiply by 9, just fold down the finger that you want to multiply by. Then the tens is on the left of the folded finger and the units on the right. For example, $9x3$, well 3 is the left middle finger, fold it down and there are two fingers to the left and 7 to the right. 27. Voila. I think and I figure out why that works. Then

- I make up a trick for eight times. Just do like the finger trick for nines, but subtract the folded finger at the end. $27 - 3 = 24 = 8*3$. Voila again, and I invented it myself, which is extra weird but even more fun than learning the tricks from someone else.

I'm not even thinking of Mrs. Finn. She thought she was punishing me, or, at least, making me do something onerous. But she is rewarding me, instead. It's fun. Because I'm weird. I know other people don't like math. I know other kids would much rather be outside running around. Or playing with friends. Or whatever it is they do. I'm happy being indoors, with no other kids, doing math.

***

I get home from school early, while Jason usually has things to do right until dinner. Mom divides the tasks: I help before dinner, he helps afterward. I learn to cook and set the table and he learns to wash dishes and clean up.

Mom is a very good cook, but she is strictly a recipe cook. Even for a dish she has made 100 times, she pulls out the recipe from her recipe box or *The Joy of Cooking* or *The New York Times Cookbook* and follows it exactly. And she makes schedules of when to start what, so that it will all come out at the right time. This method works for her and it also lets her assign particular tasks to me. One favorite is a recipe for spare ribs "Chinese style" that she got from the mom of a friend of Jason's who is Chinese. Another is a marinated leg of lamb which we call "stand up lamb" because Mom slices it and Jason and I eat faster than she slices. And potato pancakes. And chicken soup, which also yields boiled chicken that we eat with horseradish.

We barely talk while cooking, and mostly just about the cooking. She gives me all sorts of tasks to do, whatever needs doing and doesn't take too much skill. I'm not great at chopping and slicing, but I'm fine with most of the other tasks like measuring or mixing things (either by hand or in the mixer) or cooking things in a pan.

Mom and I bake once or twice a week: Brownies or chocolate cake or banana cake. We can knock any of those out in about half an hour.

Cooking with her is good; we're a good team.

***

I start to notice something: The more Dad knows about a subject, the less likely he is to give a simple answer. I know he's a lawyer, although I'm not quite sure what a lawyer does. that is. Jason and I have been to his office and know he does a lot of talking on the telephone while sitting behind his big desk, in his big office with lots of windows.

At home, if we are talking about something he knows about, his answers are full of nuance. But if we're talking about Alexander the Great, or cooking, or sports, all of which he knows nothing about, he is adamant. Just incorrect.

We've been studying ancient history. Today we learned about Alexander the Great, also known as Alexander of Macedon. At dinner, I start talking about Alexander and my father says "Macedon is in Asia Minor" and I say "No, it's north of Greece" and he says "it is across the Aegean Sea, where Turkey is now". I know I'm right! We just studied it! I jump up in the middle of dinner and go upstairs and get my atlas and check that I'm right (just to be sure). I take the atlas down to the dining room, put it on the table and say "See! Macedon is north of Greece!" And my father says "The atlas is wrong."

I'm right and he's wrong. Victory! It really feels good to be right, and it feels even better to be right against Dad, because he's Dad and because he's a genius.

***

Another thing I notice around this age is that, if I need money for something, like a lunch, it is better to ask Dad than Mom. He will give more money and then forget about it, she will give less money and ask how it was spent and want her change back.

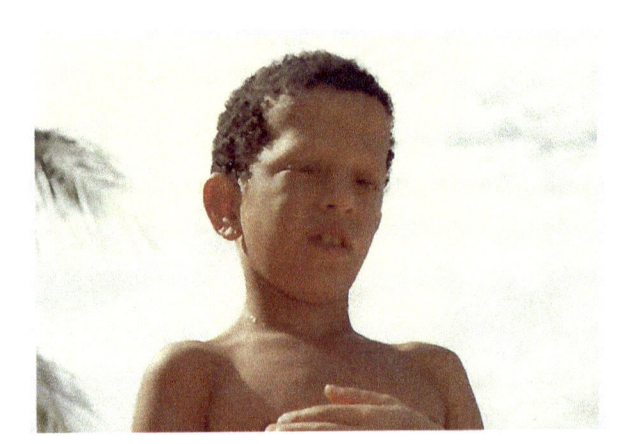

Chapter 7

Tweens

Emerson only goes through 5th grade, so it is time for a new school. We look at a few different ones and Mom decides on York Prep. I'm not sure why. Maybe because it goes through 12th grade.

I am dressed up in a white button down shirt and gray slacks and a tie and a blue blazer. Because my neck is so large and my waist and chest are so small, Mom has altered all my button down shirts to fit me. I head off to my new school for the first day of sixth grade. I'm kind of nervous and I don't like the uniform and York wasn't my first choice among the schools we toured, but I don't know which ones I got into and Mom doesn't offer me a choice, anyway.

The school is at 85th Street and Lexington Avenue. Eight blocks away. This part of Manhattan is on a grid. The school is six blocks up, two over. I have been there before, and I have the address. And ...I can't find the school.

Where the heck is the school? I'm going to be late on my first day and I *hate* being late for anything. What did it look like when I was here before? Was there an awning? Where was the number on the building? What color was the building? How close was it to the corner? I don't remember *anything*! What the heck is *wrong* with me?

Luckily, I find my way home, somehow. I've been there a whole bunch of times, which helps. I recognize the canopy with our address on it; it has a 31 on it. And it's between Madison and Fifth, even though "31 East" is usually between Madison and Park. I'm sort of aware that other people find their way home in different ways. They don't rely so much on numbers and words for directions. They recognize places. That's how they give directions, too.

I show up at the door, Mom says: "Peter! What are you doing here?"

"I can't find the school!" I tell her, crying.

She looks amazed, which just makes me feel worse. Getting lost on your way to school is surely amazing. It's amazingly stupid. So, I'm stupid. And she just doesn't get that a person, a 6th grader, could get lost this way. Just like she doesn't understand that I don't know how to make friends. Or that I can't figure out how to make a bed. Or *anything*. And *I* don't understand how people find their way around. They know where they are, somehow, in ways I don't. I don't know what this *is*, I don't know what they are doing. But they are doing something that I don't do.

Mom gives me money for a cab. I get to school about a half hour or an hour late feeling really stupid.

***

So, here I am at a new school. All the classes are easy but most of the students and some of the teachers are hard.

At Gateway, I was accepted and even had friends. At Emerson, things were going downhill, but I did have two friends. Now I'm shunned and teased and bullied and have no friends at all. Although I'm never actually beaten up, I often get shoved into trash containers; or I get glue poured in my hair. Sometimes glue gets squirted on the seat as I am about to sit down. I don't yell. I don't cry. Crying doesn't occur to me; it's not like I know not to cry, or decide not to, it just doesn't happen. I just get angrier and angrier and hold all that inside. I know I can't beat up any of my classmates. And I figure if I do yell at them or tell on them, they will beat me up. From time-to-time it all boils over and I lash out, but often at the wrong person.

Even though the classes are easy, I don't get amazing grades, although I do make the honor roll most semesters (that's just an 85 average, which is really pretty easy). The teachers say they expect an hour per night of homework per class, which would be three or four hours a night. I do about fifteen minutes total per night. Why do homework? There are books to read! And who cares if my average is 80 or 85 or 98? I do fine without bothering to study.

But it's not all bad. In sixth grade, Malcolm Spaull is my math teacher. After my tutoring experience, I had learned all of sixth grade math. After the first day of school, I take the book home and read it.

The next day I finish the in-class assignment in class in two minutes.

ME: Mr. Spaull, this is easy.
MR. S.: It gets hard later.
PETER: No, I did the whole book.
MR. S.: Come on up here.

The rest of the class is still working on the assignment I just finished in two minutes. Mr.Spaull quizzes me on sixth, seventh, and eighth grade math. I stand there by his desk while he sits. He is a very tall man and I am short, even for a sixth grader, and his head is almost even with mine. He keeps asking and I keep answering correctly.

He seems ... impressed, I guess. Or something. I'm not so much thinking about what he might be thinking or feeling. I just like solving the problems. He switches me to his ninth grade class.

In the ninth grade class, when one of the ninth graders makes mistakes in math, I say things like "This is easy. Why don't you understand it?" The ninth graders ignore me. But I say similar stuff in my regular classes and the sixth graders don't ignore me, they tease me and shun me.

***

Sometimes, the principal of the school (he calls himself "headmaster") calls me into his office when potential new parents are visiting and shows me off by asking me math questions. I feel like an animal at a livestock show. Once again I'm getting praise for stuff that is easy (like reading and math and science and standardized tests) and criticism for stuff that is hard (like making friends or being properly dressed or knowing where things are). Adults are idiots. But maybe not completely, because the parents *are* impressed at this scrawny, short, 6th grader doing high school math.

I am miserable. I am bored. I am very angry and also pretty verbally adept. That's a bad combination.

Kids are forming groups, somehow. Getting together. Making friends and more than friends. I think. Sort of. Some kids are more than friends. Some of it is sex, I mean, I know there are boys and girls and stuff. Girls are different. And boys talk about girls differently. About what they do with girls, or want to do. I certainly want to do different stuff with girls than boys, but I am clueless. But some of what is going on is just some weird thing called friendship. I don't know. I get shunned, I don't know why; I don't even know from what. People point and laugh when I enter the room or when they see me outside of class.

***

I am 11 years old. I am sitting in my room playing math, which is one of the best games ever. I'm doing some of it in my head, and some with paper and pen. I've just learned about the Fibonacci numbers. This is a very famous series of numbers. It works like this: Start with two 1s. Then, each number is the sum of the previous two. Like this: $1, 1, 2, 3, 5, 8, 13\ldots$

A lot of the neat things about this series are about the ratios of a term to the previous term:

- $1/1 = 1$
- $2/1 = 2$
- $3/2 = 1.5$
- $5/3 = 1.666\ldots$
- $8/5 = 1.6$
- $13/8 = 1.625$
- $\ldots$

I read that these quickly converge to a number that is called the golden ratio or ϕ and that has a lot of cool attributes. But I'm playing math, not just learning, so I play and pick different starting numbers. I try all sorts of different starting numbers. And add. And divide. And, no matter what numbers I pick, the ratio always converges. Fast. To the same thing. For instance, I start with -1002 and 56 and that gives a series
$-1002, 56, -946, -890, -1836, -2726, -4562\ldots$
and $\frac{-4562}{-2726} = 1.673$

And that is so cool.

But math is about more than showing things, you have to prove them. So I do. At least, to my own satisfaction. I am excited to show Mr. Spaull what I've done. He is impressed but points out that out that this was proven many years ago. Still, I did it.

But it's weird that I think this is fun. Normal kids don't like math.

***

I'm about to turn 12 and I'm still wetting the bed. Because I so rarely sleep at other kids' houses, I only slowly become aware that this is weird. Jason stopped years ago. My parents have tried everything. No water after dinner. Waking me up a couple times in the night. Making me change my own sheets, which is kind of annoying but makes a certain sense. Nothing works. I wonder why they make such a big deal of it. But I also wonder why I am weird and wet the bed at age 11. They do get a special sheet to protect the mattress, so it's less stinky, but nothing works.

And then, one night, my brain figures it out. I have a nightmare. I dream that I am in a car with a bunch of people, these aren't people I know in real life, but we are all colleagues of some sort in the dream, and we are all adults. We are driving on a mountain road, when there's a landslide and, as the rocks are about to hit our car and I'm about to die, I wake up. I go to the bathroom and pee. I go back to sleep. I wake up dry. This feels good and mom is happy to see dry sheets. And the next night I wake up dry again and the next. And so on. The good feeling builds until it stops mattering because it is now normal, not just for 12 year olds, but for me.

***

We've moved to a new apartment on 79th street. It is a triplex! Sixth, seventh, and eighth floor. On the sixth floor, there is a foyer, the kitchen, the dining room, and the living room. On the seventh is our parents' bedroom and a den. And Jason and I have the top floor more or less to ourselves, except for the laundry room. Even though there are two large bedrooms, we decide to share a room and use the extra room for other things. There's also a tiny bedroom that some guests use. And there's five bathrooms! There's one in my parents' bedroom that has two mirrors facing each other, so you can see an endless stream of you; the one in the den has a shower with five nozzles and a steam bath; there's a normal one in the room I share with Jason, and a little one in the foyer, and a tiny one up on the third floor in the back.

The kitchen is long and narrow, with the dishwasher at one end and most of the cupboards at the other. My mother, of course, has bought a special tray just to load and carry dishes from the dishwasher. She fills every square inch of it on each trip through the kitchen. She has rules for herself that she tries to impose on us, such as never going from one room to another empty-handed, or leaving things on the edge of the stairwell when they have to go up or down.

One time, Mom gets Dad to unload the dishwasher. Ordinarily, he doesn't do anything around the house; I never saw him operate a vacuum cleaner, load a load of laundry, or make a bed. But he's in the kitchen when Mom is too and the dishwasher is full and she asks him to unload it while she is cleaning up after dinner. He opens the dishwasher, takes out a plate, closes the dishwasher, carries the plate to the cupboard, puts it away, closes the cupboard, walks all the way down the kitchen and repeats the whole procedure again and again. I see mom getting angrier and angrier. I forget if she even let him finish, but she never asked him again.

We eat dinner each night at exactly 6:30. If Dad is home, we eat in the dining room, otherwise, we eat in the kitchen. When we eat in the kitchen, I sit nearest the phone. Many nights, right at 6:30, the phone rings and, as I pick up the phone, Mom says "Tell him I know he's not home and I don't care when he gets here." Then we have dinner. This happens so often it almost becomes a joke. If the phone rings right at 6:30, I know it's Dad, and I know Mom's reaction, and the whole thing is kind of funny.

She must know whether he will be coming home before he calls, because the choice of room had to be made. But how does she know? I'm guessing she made a deal with Dad's secretary.

Another feature of the kitchen is a poster Mom bought that says "Write all complaints in the box below" in big letters and then there is a tiny box, about 1/2 inch on each side.

***

There is going to be a science fair. I'm doing a project on probability. It's titled "How the Dice will Roll." I first figure out the probability of every total from rolling two dice. For example, a total of 2 will happen $\frac{1}{36}$ of the time, but a total of 7 will happen $\frac{6}{36} = \frac{1}{6}$ of the time, because there are six ways to get a total of 7 (1-6, 6-1, 2-5, 5-2, 3-4, and 4-3). Figuring this stuff out is fun.

I turn that into a chart, then I roll dice a whole bunch of times. Rolling the dice over and over is boring, but I figure that it is part of the process and I've read about the tedious parts of science and math. Gauss, for example, made his own tables of various functions. I let my parents help only in the actual rolling of the dice. One of them will roll and I will note the result in a tally. Anything more would be cheating, at least to me, even if I know that other kids are getting help from their parents. And I don't *want* their help. I don't want to let them do things for me. I don't want more time with them. And I don't want to owe them any favors.

Then I make a graph comparing my prediction to what actually happened. I put the different possible results on the horizontal axis, and the number of times it happened on the y axis. I make a bar for each actual result and I put dots for my predicted results, I connect the dots with lines.

The dots are pretty close to the bars! That's so cool! I carry my posters to school; it's just kids and teachers, not parents. My set up is pretty easy, since it's just two posters that I put on stands. Other kids have to set up fake volcanoes or whatever. I look around at I see what other kids are doing and they are all doing stupid, boring stuff. The volcano thing is in every book! I figure I'm sure to win.

I don't win. After the prizes are awarded, one teacher tells me they didn't understand what I had done. The winner was some kid who made a poster about his snake, which he brought in its cage.

Jeeze. You'd think they would pick judges who could understand what 6th graders are doing! I mean, my project is cool and all, but it's not all that hard and they are adults! Adults are, once again, stupid.

***

Another teacher I like somewhat is Mr. Linton. He is a short, slender man from the South. I think he mentions he's from Alabama. He teaches us English, where he does pretty well. He also teaches sex ed., which is kind of comical, as he can not get himself to say such words as "penis" or "vagina" or "intercourse" or even "sex". So, we learn about the development of the fetus, but not how it gets there.

***

I gradually become aware that other kids are cheating off me. I figure if I let them do it, maybe they'll like me. This doesn't work, they still don't like me. I never cheat off anyone else. Not only does that offend my sense of myself, but I am sure I would get caught.

***

I am in 7th grade, my second year at York, the class play is *Our Town* by Thornton Wilder. I am cast as Howie the milkman. On the way to the performance, I'm crossing Madison Avenue to get to school. I see a cab a couple blocks down Madison, going pretty fast, but I have the green light so I head across the street. Then bam! I'm hit and I go flying through the air (I found out later that the driver's brakes had failed). Then I'm in an ambulance. I can't move and I'm scared that I might be dead or something, but then I remember that I read somewhere that you can't imagine something you've never seen before (this isn't correct, but it still calms me down). Then I'm in the hospital. Doctors and nurses are standing over me asking me stupid questions like "What's your name?" Then my mom shows up with some guy who I've never met. She also tells me that my pediatrician, Dr. Bauer, is away. She tells me he is her doctor, Dr. Hitzig. He starts asking questions.

DR HITZIG: Who's the president?
ME: Nixon.
DR. HITZIG: Is he a good president?
ME: No.
DR. HITZIG, TO MY MOM: If he had said yes—back in the coma!

Mom tells me that I landed on my head at the feet of a nurse who was on her way to Mt. Sinai and that I had a concussion and was unconscious for a couple of hours, but not in a coma. But Mom and I still both like Dr. Hitzig's joke.

That evening, the nurse comes to visit and check up on me, which is very nice. I am in the hospital for two days when Mom insists I be let go, even though the doctors think I should stay a little longer. A couple months later, I get a payment from the insurance, it was a lot of money for a 7th grader! I find out that there is a standard payment per day in the hospital and I get mad at Mom. "Why did you get me out early? I could have made more money!" The hospital was kind of boring, but not so bad: I had books. And the nurses were very nice to me.

***

I am going to have eye surgery. I've had bad eyes since birth. I see out of only one eye at a time, using my right eye for anything less than two feet away and my left for everything else. My right eye wanders so much that sometimes only the white is visible. I've been seeing eye doctors once or twice a year since I was a baby, I even had eye surgery when I was three to try and get my eyes to work together. Now, they want to do cosmetic surgery that will make it look like my eyes are both focusing. This sounds good to me, at least I will look less weird. The surgeon is Philip Knapp and I think that he has an amazing number of P's in his name. He works at Harkness Eye Pavilion, way uptown. Every time we go see him it's a long bus ride on the number 4 bus, up Madison Avenue.

The day of surgery arrives. I'm in the hospital for a couple days. After the surgery both my eyes are bandaged and Mom reads to me sometimes, but I'm very bored. And the food stinks. Then they take the bandages off and, as expected, my vision hasn't changed but my eyes look much better.

> *The car crash and the eye surgery happened at around the same time, but ... I don't remember which happened first and, at this point, there's no one left alive who can tell me. I sort of think that the eye surgery was first. But I don't really know. And my thinking this is based on thinking, not on the sort of sense of time that most people seem to have.*
>
> *I think this is related to my NLD, I've heard of this sort of thing in some other people with NLD, but it's not the center of the diagnosis. It happens with more minor life events too. I don't remember when things happened, or in what order they happened.*

I've survived being hit by a cab, having eye surgery, and 7th grade, but will I survive 8th grade?

***

I am 12 years old. Nancy is getting married to an architect from Chicago named Richard Solomon who we all call Rick. They met while he was in graduate school but now he is working. He's a really nice guy with brown hair and a beard and a mustache. He even likes math! And he collects these really tiny model soldiers, which he paints in individual uniforms with the tiniest paint brushes I've ever seen. I can't imagine painting like that, but I like the information about the soldiers so, when he is in New York, he sometimes takes me to the Soldier Shop, which is right near our apartment. While he examines soldiers, I read the books that have all sorts of detailed information on uniforms and so on.

It's Super Bowl Sunday, but instead of watching the game in the den in my usual clothes, I'm wearing an uncomfortable button down shirt and an uncomfortable suit and holding a pole in the ballroom of the Pierre Hotel. The pole is one of four that is holding up the chuppa at Nancy and Rick's wedding. (In a Jewish wedding, the bride and groom get married under a canopy called a chuppa, which is held up by four poles, each held by a person close to the couple).

My parents don't think I am a good choice. They're worried that I might wander off in the middle, letting the canopy fall on the bride and groom, but, Nancy wants Jason and me to each hold a pole. This time, she insists. I can see all my elder relatives are watching me, ready to jump in if I wander off. While holding the pole and also watching Nancy in her white gown coming down the aisle, and also Rick standing and waiting, I think about math problems . Our rabbi Michael leads the wedding and then there is "I do".

After the ceremony, Rick takes Jason and me up to the bridal suite, where we watch the game. I'm not that into football, but this is certainly better than standing around in uncomfortable clothes. Nancy is downstairs with the guests, of course, and Rick rejoins her after getting us settled.

I don't remember the game, not even who played or who won. But I remember holding the pole. I know Mom would have said it shouldn't be me and I know Nancy stood up for me, so I stood up for her. And I didn't wander off or let the pole fall or anything. I felt like a grown up. And I felt good.

***

Chapter 8

Early Teens

I am about to turn 13 and Mom wants me to go to summer camp for a month. I don't want to go. I want to stay in my room all summer, with a big pile of books and come out for meals and baths. But Mom wants me to go to camp. She wants me to be social. She tells me I will make friends. The only people I want to be social with are my siblings and their friends, and with adults. But Mom wants me to be social so I go to camp.

I hate it. I'm not homesick. Can you be roomsick? I want to be in my room. Alone. Introverts don't belong at summer camp. I don't pitch a tantrum, but I make it clear that I would be happy alone in my room.

I'm weird. I like math and science and music written before I was born. I don't like sports and I don't like camping and I don't like sleeping in a room full of kids. I'm so skinny that some kids think I might be malnourished. Then they see me eat. I like to read the almanac, especially the tables of numbers, which I play with and make charts. When my brother and I play Strato-Matic baseball, I figure the odds of each thing happening (this was determined by rolling dice). Now, *that* is fun. And I am weird.

When the other kids play baseball or whatever, I lie on the grass and read. Other kids make fun of me and, usually, the counsellors do nothing about it.

> *We try a different camp each summer and I hate them all. Mom asks me about each camp and whether I liked it, but it never occurs to her that what had made her happy as a kid would not make me happy, or that what made her miserable as a kid would make me happy. Not just particular activities, but entire ways of being. She's an extrovert, she often has friends over, there are dinner parties and lots of being around other people. I am an extreme introvert, She doesn't get it. Looking back, she probably also got notes from the camps, saying I didn't really belong there, but, unlike the note from Rudolf Steiner school, she didn't save these, or, at least, never showed them to me.*

Every day at camp, even the first day, I get a letter from my mom. A long letter, carefully composed, I can tell, and signed "Love, Mom". And, in four years at camp, I get one letter from Dad, typed by his secretary and signed "Sincerely, Joe." Somehow I know that he didn't really mean it. That's just him. I send back letters saying things like

> Dear Mom and Dad,
> I am fine, they made me write or they wouldn't let me eat.
> Love, Peter

But, even as I write that, I wonder if I love them and I know I'm not fine.

When I get home, Mom gets mad at me. She has had my room painted while I was away and I haven't noticed. Hey! It's the same color as before! Just fresh paint. Who notices that? OK, probably most people. But why did she think I would? Why does she think

I'm like her? She's lived with me for a decade, and she just doesn't get it at all. OK, if you asked her "Claire, is your son just like you?" of course she'd say "no." But she doesn't get it. It's not just that she wishes I was more like her, it's that she hasn't figured out the ways that I'm not.

***

I am 13 years old and have just become a bar mitzvah. Although I was born in July, we are celebrating in September, after the Jewish New Year, both so that more people can come (since many of my friends and my parents' friends would be away in July) and so that I read from the first book of Genesis. Even though I'm already an atheist, the first book of Genesis is kind of cool to read.

Both the ceremony and the celebration are happening right at home. It's a fairly small group of guests, since I don't have friends from school and since I insisted that the only friends of my parents who can come are the ones I really like. Still, it involved a considerable transformation of the apartment. The ceremony is in the living room, in front of the non-working fireplace, with all the furniture gone. Lunch is served on rented tables in the living room, dining room, and den. Further partying is in the living room and dining room for the grownups, and on the third floor for the kids.

The ceremony is over, the party is done, the guests have gone. Only my parents and Nancy and Jason are left and I'm opening presents. Money. Toys. One person gives me stock. One person buys me a tree in Israel. The best gift is from my sister. Her present is about the size of a piece of paper, but much thicker and heavier. I rip off the wrapping paper. It's a calculator! Just what I wanted.

Me and the calculator, Jason is in the background

It has four functions. It has a memory. You have to plug it into the wall for it to work. It weighs about five pounds and it cost around $100. [1]

I love it. I immediately start playing with it. I don't even think to tell Nancy how it's the best gift; even better than the slide rule that Dad bought me a few years ago for my birthday, and way better than any toy. Nancy's not a math person. But she knows her little brother and knows he likes math (and Rick, her husband, may have helped pick it out, Rick knows stuff like this).

Not only do I use it to help with things like math homework,

---

[1] In 1972. That would be about $700 today.

but I play with it. Look!

$1234 * 9 = 11106$.

And look what I discovered: Start with any string of consecutive digits and multiply by 9 and you get a string of 1's, then a 0, then a digit.

$12345 * 9 = 1111104$

Isn't that *cool*? I think it is, that's for sure! And if you add up the number of 1's and the digit at the end, you always get 9! It's way cooler than anything any athlete or musician does. And I have to know *why*. And what happens if you extend the string of digits? Or skip one? I never share these cool results with anyone, but that doesn't matter. I know. That's enough.

***

All through my childhood I actually *like* hanging out with adults. And with babies. But not my peers. A lot of big kids are really mean. Little kids don't even think about being mean; they might be rude, but that's different. When a three year old says "I hate you" they aren't being mean, exactly, they are just stating their opinion of the moment, using the words that they have. And adults, at least nice adults, deliberately refrain from being mean. Being mean is rude. It's only big kids who are able to be mean and not reluctant to be so.

> *One friend of my parents met me when I was 13 at a dinner party my parents threw. She much later told me that when she first saw me there, she wondered what my parents were thinking, but when I started talking, she knew I belonged. What kind of kid hates gym and art and likes math? Well, me! And there are others like me, but they don't go to the schools my mother sends me to.*

***

I'm 13 and in 8th grade at York. It's not getting any better. I'm miserable and, therefore, I'm obnoxious to many of my teachers. One day I'm sitting in social studies class, calling out answers and other things without raising my hand.

MS. EPPS: Peter, be quiet.
ME: I don't have to listen to you because I am smarter than you.

She turns red and starts crying and has to leave the room. I feel good and bad at the same time. Ms. Epps is a pretty nice woman and a pretty good teacher. But I have power. And I use it.

***

I know when I'm being mean to teachers. It's deliberate. Some teachers deserve it (like Mrs. Buglion) others don't (like Ms. Epps) but I am mean more-or-less indiscriminately. When I get mad enough, I get mean. And I am unfortunately good at it. And the same thing happens with kids. I don't vent my anger most strongly at the kids who are meanest, it's more or less random. And then I often feel bad, if the kid or teacher wasn't an appropriate target. My skill at insulting people makes these feelings worse.

I attend classes with the same small group of people, year after year York has tracking and I'm in the "fast" track for everything. Each grade has the grade number and then another number for the track, like 6-1, 6-3 and so on. They try to hide the tracking by sometimes making the second number reversed, so 6-1 is the smart track in 6th grade and 7-4 is the smart track in 7th grade. This fools no one, of course, as the same kids move from one grade to the next. Everyone knows which the smart class is, regardless of how they label the groups. It's the one with me and Ellen and Philip and Neal and Ottilie and so on.

After school I often have detention, mostly for talking out of turn, interrupting, or being rude to teachers. (One day, I have detention from all four classes that I had that day (you can't get detention from gym or lunch). After school (with or without detention) I go home and read until dinner time (and sometimes, maybe, I do some homework).

I don't see detention as punishment. Instead of reading at home, I read in a classroom. I don't have friends, so I don't miss hanging out with them. There are only a few clubs, none that I'm interested in. There are sports teams, but I hate sports and stink at them (I'm OK at swimming but there is no swimming team and York doesn't have a pool). And, since detention is pretty closely supervised, I don't get teased or bullied while I am there. When I ask kids to sign my yearbook they put things like "Dear Martian..."

Everyone knows me. They all know I am weird and make fun of me for being weird. I'm the kid who interrupts and sometimes corrects the teacher, I'm the kid who likes math and hates gym. They roll their eyes at me. I've stopped getting shoved into trash cans (I don't fit any more) but the glue incidents continue.

And because it is such a small school and goes from 6th to 12th grades, every dorky or dopey thing I do follows me. It's not so much specific incidents that follow me, as the general impression that I am definitely weird.

Now that Nancy and Rick are living in Chicago, I regularly take my Thanksgiving, Christmas, and spring vacations in Chicago, at their apartment. No matter how many times I go to LaGuardia Airport, I always allow too much time and get there too early. On my first few trips, Nancy meets me at the airport in Chicago, but then I learn to take a cab by myself.

These trips are wonderful. Nancy is still Nancy and Rick is a mensch. In the day times, when Rick is at work, Nancy and I talk about all sorts of things, such as politics and our family. When Rick is around, I sometimes talk to him about more technical things; he can understand the joy of math, which Nancy can't. But, more than any specific thing, when I'm with Nancy and Rick there is a feeling of being welcome and being loved and being listened to.

Nancy offers to let me come stay with them. It's tempting. They have plenty of space, and I could probably go to the same school where Rick went. We talk about it—things like where I would go to school and so on—but I never really get serious about it. I don't know how I would tell Mom. How would it go:

PETER: Hey mom? I've decided to move to Chicago and live with Rick and Nancy.
MOM: Why?
PETER: Because Nancy is a much better mother than you are, and actually knows how to show that she loves me.

I don't have the guts for that, sadly.

What I should have said, when Nancy asked, "Hey Nancy? I accept. I want to move to Chicago and move in with you and Rick. Our mom can't mother me. She doesn't know how. And I'm suicidal a lot and here's a poem I wrote and why do you get me but our mom doesn't? And how did you figure out how to do that? And I know I want to be a dad someday, and I want to learn from you and Rick and not Mom and Dad. And I want to play on computers with Rick and have tickle wars with Jonathan and eat dinner every night where dinner isn't a battle for supremacy and where people can express love for one another and where hugging is common and crying isn't rare and signs of affection happen all the time. I want to watch Aaron and Jonathan grow up at first hand, and baby sit for them when you go out. I want to go to Francis Parker instead of York Prep.

But, anyway, thank you so much for your offer and I think it will save my life. Now ... how do we tell Mom?

Part II

Nadir

Chapter 9

Ledge revisited

I am 14 years old, in ninth grade, my third year at York. I am weird and this is no fun. What's wrong is not so much a thing as an absence of things. It's not even the absence of any one thing. It's not just that I have no friends, nor that most of my teachers have no clue what to do with me. It's not just that my father is rarely home since he works 80 or 90 hours a week. It's not just that my mom is home all the time, but emotionally absent. It's not just that Nancy is in Chicago nor that Sabha's Mom moved them to Dublin last year.

It's not just that I get bullied every day nor that I get in trouble with at least one teacher almost every day.

It's all of that.

Then there is me. I'm broken. I'm defective. And there isn't even a proper name for my defect. At least I've substituted "learning disabled" for "minimal brain dysfunction", even if I never get the diagnosis changed officially. But *what* learning disability? No one at York calls me "learning disabled" anyway. The teachers call me lazy or say I am not paying attention; the students call me "weirdo" or "spazzo" or such.

As I get older, my peers are more and more willing to let me know that I am broken and my teachers don't step in to stop it.

CHAPTER 9. LEDGE REVISITED

The many times I got stuffed into trash cans, I just pulled myself out. Bullying is, after all, normal, and boys will be boys. Eighth grade was worse than seventh, which was worse than sixth, and all the way back. I wonder if it will keep getting worse.

Nothing is new this year, but everything is more intense. The name calling gets more inventive; the shunning gets more active and now there's a romantic element. Boys don't want to be my friend and girls certainly don't want to be my girlfriend. Even the good parts of my weirdness become targets; kids sometimes call me "brainiac" but it doesn't feel like a compliment. People laugh at me or point at me on the street outside school.

One way I'm broken is that I don't know why any of this is happening. Since I don't know why anything is happening, I have no idea how to fix it. I have no agency. I'm completely confused by everything in school that isn't actual school work.

Each morning I get up, eat breakfast, and am off to school. I go to whatever classes I have that day; I sit in the same seat I always do and, inevitably, call out answers out of turn (and call out whatever else comes to mind—my mind races and I have very little impulse control). Sometimes I do my homework for the classes I have later that day.

People seem to look at me oddly a lot. In gym, I sit on the side and read while the class plays basketball or whatever; no one particularly cares. There are too many kids in class to all play basketball at once anyway. For lunch, we all go out to buy our lunch and I often wind up taking my lunch back to school and eating alone, or sitting alone in Blimpies with my giant sandwich. After the last class there is usually detention, sometimes with other kids. I usually have detention for being rude to the teacher, or calling out answers or random things.

Then I go home, have a snack, and read until it's time to help Mom make dinner. Then dinner. Then I read some more, or watch TV until bed.

And there's always a sort of drone note: Why stay alive? Once in a while I actively think about suicide, but the question "why stay alive?" is always there in the background.

I don't have a good answer to that. I can't stop asking the question. Tonight, the drone note in my head gets too loud and I can't stop the active thinking; the idea of suicide seems better and better and the idea of staying alive seems pointless. So I climb out on the ledge and think about falling down those 8 floors onto the unknown ground.

But I can always kill myself tomorrow, so, back into my room I go.

Part III

Rise

Chapter 10

Ages 15 and 16

Since I decided to come in off the ledge, things begin to change, but slowly.

Today is super snowy (but not enough to close the schools), a lot of kids are absent so Ms. Epps, decides to hold a debate. We are studying World War II and the debate question is "Could Hitler have arisen in any country other than Germany?"

I start thinking about the issues in the few minutes between when Ms. Epps announced the question and the debate started: National characteristics of different people, the dire economic situation in Germany, resentment after the Versailles treaty ending WW I, that sort of thing. The other kids are sitting in their seats, snickering, rolling their eyes at me, the alien in their midst. They look bored. That sucks, but it's also weird. Why aren't they interested? It's a really interesting question! I don't even know which side I favor: *Could* Hitler have arisen in France or the USA or England or the Soviet Union or whatever?

Ms. Epps asks "Who wants to argue for the 'yes' side?" I raise my hand (no one else does). Then she asks "How about the 'no' side?" And ... no one raises their hand so, after a while, I do. I debate myself. I sit there and argue one side. Then I argue against what I just said. Back and forth. It's wonderful fun, even if the other kids are agog at this new evidence of weirdness.

If York had had a debate team, that would have been good.

***

One teacher I particularly dislike is my 8th grade English teacher, Mrs. Buglion. Her class is boring and ridiculously easy and she is kind of old and very old fashioned. I always sit in her class doing crossword puzzles. After I do this a few times, she says: "Peter, either put those away or go to the Dean's office." I get up and leave, because I don't really want to be in class. I start to go to the Dean's office, but then I think he will probably punish me somehow, or make me go back to class, and I don't want that. What's the worst that could happen if I don't go? Detention? I don't mind detention. Suspension seems unlikely. So, I go to the library and read and do crosswords until it's time for the next class.

But she never checks, so, I keep doing crossword in class and she keeps throwing me out and I keep going to the library. It's great! It's like playing hooky with the teacher's permission! If I ever did play hooky, I'd sit home and read. But now I get to do it in the library. A whole room full of books!

Then I get very high marks on all the tests she gives us all year, except spelling. I'm actually a really good speller, but my handwriting is a huge handicap; she can't read my writing so I get them wrong, even if the word is correct (in fairness to her, I've seen my handwriting. No one could read it). My good marks further infuriate her! She practically slams my test papers down on my desk as if to say: "How dare you learn the subject without being in class much of the time, or paying attention when you are?"

Ah, power again, at least, the power to infuriate her. Some teachers are just clueless.

In the spring, she decides to hold a spelling bee. Since I always get bad grades on spelling tests, she probably figures I will mess up early. As she keeps calling out words, different kids get them wrong and sit down. I keep getting them right. I'm the last one standing. She doesn't declare me the winner, she keeps trying to stump me. And even then, she can't stump me before the class is over. The last word she calls out is "schwa", which I also get.

She is such an idiot and it feels so good to prove it to her (and to my classmates, even though they probably don't care).

***

Browsing in a book store (a habit of mine) I see *The Juggling Book* by Carlo in a book store. I buy it and decide to teach myself to juggle. It takes me many hours of practice alone in my room to learn even the basic three ball cascade. But so what? I eventually get it. And it feels great to be able to do it and to have *learned* to do it. I am finally successful at something that is hard for me!

I show my parents and Jason and they are amazed that I can do it. I am a klutz. Later, I show other people, including classmates, but they seem less impressed.

Once I get a little better I go buy juggling equipment at a store and studio downtown. Along with my purchases, I find juggling groups, full of interesting people. I hear about one group that meets in Washington Square Park in nice weather and in the studio in the winter. I take the subway to the park and find the group. There's no official welcome or anything, it's a very loose and relaxed group. There are some people who are just beginning and don't even juggle yet, but are being taught. Someone says "Hey, do you juggle?" and I say "a little" and I take out some beanbags and juggle. And I stop to watch the experts, who do remarkable things.

Some are professionals, some are buskers, and most (like me) just do it for fun. Some do other circus arts, like tight rope walking. But we all do it together. And no one makes fun of me, even if it takes me a lot longer to learn a trick than it took them. In this world, quirkiness is not only tolerated, but welcomed; these are quirky people. They aren't circus people, exactly, because they don't belong to a circus. But they are definitely living lives that are very atypical.

Tony Duncan is the best of this group, he is a real professional juggler who gives shows regularly and teaches group lessons, more or less for free. He will just see someone struggling with a trick and show them how to do it.

Lots of jugglers like to juggle in pairs or groups They offer to teach me. From the start, it is really joyous. This is usually done with clubs rather than balls or beanbags and it feels amazing! At first, we do very basic, regular patterns, but, as I get better, we mix the pattern up. I'm guessing this is what singing or playing an instrument in a jazz group feels like. There's a base but there is lots of room for improvisation.

When it gets colder, the group moves into a studio. Tony offers semi-formal classes; mostly it's about juggling, but there's a guy named Marcel who is an expert on physical comedy and can fall down funny. And one young woman is great on the tight rope.

I even go to a jugglers' convention a few times. They are held in big gyms with high ceilings. And not only does no one make fun of me, no one makes fun of anyone. Here are jugglers from the best in the world down to people who have never juggled before, and yet, everyone welcomes everyone.

***

It's June. I'm in Spanish class and today is the final exam. The teacher passes out the test and I decide it's a dumb test, full of fill-in-the-blank questions and other things that I don't think test us on anything useful. I yell "This is a dumb test and I'm not going to take it!" Then I tear it up and fling the shreds on the floor, then I storm out of the room. Since it's final exam time, I just leave the school since I had no other exams that day.

I am waiting to get yelled at by my parents, but it doesn't happen. The school didn't 't even tell them! What is *wrong* with the teacher? But my parents don't really punish me for stuff, even if they are aware of it. I don't know what they would do. They don't believe in hitting me, they aren't going to deny me food, sending me to my room would be a reward. Maybe no dessert. So what?

Naturally, I get an F on the test, which is almost cool. My parents express disappointment, but nothing more. Then, a few months later, I'm ahead of the most advanced class in Spanish (not that this meant much).

In chemistry, one kid cheats off me in chemistry. He gets a 100 when I get a 98! That pisses me off and I stop letting people do it. It never worked for making friends, anyway.

I don't have friends at York, or outside of it. But I do have some friends by proxy. My brother is an extrovert. He makes friends. He makes himself charming and he tolerates a lot in people who want to be his friends. One of his friends is a kleptomaniac, when he sleeps over, we sleep with our wallets under our pillows. Sometimes his friends come to our house, and I can hang out with them. Sometimes we play poker with lots of wild cards and very low stakes. Sometimes they go out to dinner and I go along. A couple times I'm invited along to parties (whether by the host or by Jason).

This is new. Until now, I've been aware, more-or-less, of his friends. But now I'm part of the group, if only on the periphery. And I don't partake in all their activities. A bunch of them are musicians, or want to be. My brother forms a band and they practice in his room. I wander over to his room to help them set up, but I don't play; I have no musical talent. They all drink and do drugs, but I don't. I do get a kind of contact drunk. When my brother and his friends are drunk, I act like a bit like they do.

Jason's friend Tim is a nice enough kid, but we have very little in common. Tonight, when a bunch of Jason's friends are over, Tim wanders into my room and looks at my books. I already have one whole wall lined with bookcases, and some overflow.

TIM: Wow. Have you read all these?
PETER: Well, most of them. Not the reference books.

TIM: Wow. Wow.

He wanders out of my room back to my brother's. And I wonder about people who don't read. I am reminded that most teenagers don't read 4 or 5 hours a day. They don't just come home and read until dinner, and then read until bed.

One night, I'm lying on the floor in Jason's room and two of his friends (a boy and a girl) are yelling at each other. Then, for some reason, they go into the bathroom, one at a time. They come out naked. Seeing a live girl naked is a big deal; so far, the only naked women I've seen are in Playboy. The girl is nice looking, but not like Playboy. But live is better; when she comes out of the bathroom I get a full view. Then they make love in front of me on my brother's bed. I'm not sure if they know I'm there or if they just don't care. I wonder why they don't ask me to leave. I wonder how they went from fighting to having sex.

I watch, but not too intently. The sex itself isn't much to watch, I can't really tell what is going on. but when she lies down, most of her is hidden. I know they probably shouldn't be doing this in front of me, I wonder if they are even aware of me, I wonder if I should get up and leave. But I don't.

***

My brother and I like to go to Aqueduct or Belmont and bet on horses. A few years ago, my father introduced Jason and me to the joy of thoroughbred racing at Aqueduct and Belmont Race tracks. We would go on a weekend when the weather was good and sit in the nicer section of the stands, although the main difference seemed to be the price of the seats and the degree of crowding. He would give us each a little money to bet with, I think he gave us each $2 per race, which was the minimum you could bet. We were too young to place bets, so Dad would bet for us. Dad got pretty involved, he even owned a piece of a racehorse, Mr. CH. It was fun. Dad actually relaxed a bit; an entire hour might go by without him getting on a pay phone to make a call and charge it to his credit card. He can say his card number really fast, from practice.

Our trips there stopped when Mom forbade them. She just told him not to do it any more, saying it was teaching us to gamble. He didn't argue, at least, not in front of me. He just stopped.

But now, my brother and I go a lot (without Dad), Jason goes more than I do. He often cuts school to go; I only go on weekends and vacations. Tim's father, Connie, writes a tip sheet at the track. On weekends, he drives us to the track; he plays classical music loudly on the radio (he used to play bassoon for the New York Philharmonic) and curses at other drivers. Tim sits in the front seat next to his father and Jason and I sit in the back. There's always lots of chatter among four guys.

We bet. I bet moderate amounts and mostly on a single horse winning (but sometimes on other bets). Betting is pleasantly risky, but I have no urge to bet a lot. I study handicapping, read books, and buy the *Racing Form* even when I'm not going to the track. For me, it's fun, and studying and calculating is part of the fun. Jason is differently wired. He bets more than he can afford and bases his bets on no research at all and often on higher risk exotic bets. But he is good to be around, even when he is losing. He never stops being him, in so many ways unlike me, which provides a lot of what I am missing.

***

When our parents go away on trips, we have parties. Whenever they go away, Mom tells our doormen not to let anyone but us into the apartment, but the doormen like us a lot more than they like her, so, we have parties and they never tell.

One time, a party gets a bit out of control in terms of number of people and about 50 people wind up sleeping in the apartment. People are sleeping all over. One person is sleeping on the stairs.

And I'm a part of all this at one remove. None of them are my friends, but I'm the host's brother. The really nice thing is that no one sleeps in my room. I don't even have to say anything, somehow, my room is off limits. Maybe Jason told people, which would have been nice of him.

Sometimes, when our parents are away, we move all the furniture out of the living room so my brother's band can rehearse. There are chairs and tables and a big couch that can seat four people and must weigh a few hundred pounds. We put most of it in the foyer, and some in the dining room.

Our parents have been away for a week. It's been a wild week, with lots of band practices and parties. The apartment is a mess. There are ashes in all the cigarette holders, the sheets are all over the house, everything is dirty, and Mom is amazingly good at finding things that are out of place. Our parents are due back this weekend. On Friday, Jason and I hurry back from our separate schools, along with some of Jason's friends, knowing that we have to spend hours cleaning up and straightening up. It would have been easier if we had all stayed in Jason's rooms, or, at least, just done band practice in the living room and done the drinking and smoking and partying elsewhere but high and drunk teenagers are not known for that sort of thinking, and, while I was sober, I certainly wasn't going to object to anything. I was part of the gang, even if on the periphery, and I wasn't about to risk that. Helping my brother out is cool. Fooling our mom is cool too. And, I did get a sort of contact drunk and contact high.

When we get home, expecting to see the foyer full of furniture, all the furniture has been moved back into the living room, including the huge couch. And the living room has a deep, plush rug. Carmen, our cleaning lady (Jason and I call her the brown tornado), is working away but stops when we come in.

"Carmen" Jason asks, "how did the couch get back in the living room?" "I push!" she says.

***

Despite the drugs and the alcohol and the cutting school, Jason is doing fine at Fieldston. He cheats a lot and tells me about it. One story he has told a few times is how, in a Russian history class, he got his friend Nick to write a paper for him. He didn't even know what it was about. When the professor handed the papers back, she said "you did a great job with Nicholas." Jason thinks he's really in trouble, but it turns out the paper was about Czar Nicholas. He also hires a guy to write some papers.

I am clueless about most of what he does. Sure, I know he is doing a lot of drugs and drinking, I know he is cheating, but, when I think about it at all, I figure it's normal and fine. His friends are mostly doing similar things and I don't know what my peers are doing. He's Jason. That's what Jason does.

Me? I wouldn't cheat, but even if I wanted to. Even if I had a friend to ask, how would I do it? And how would I find someone to write a paper for me for money? I am clueless.

> *Much later, I realize that he was putting himself in real danger. Not just from the usual dangers of drugs, but because he is allergic to nuts and could die if he eats one, which he might do while stoned. But back when we were both teens, I didn't think about it because I didn't have any frame of reference.*

***

Some of my parents' friends like me. In particular, Gershon and Carol Kekst (Gershon is client of my father), and Ira and Phyllis Wender (Ira has been a friend of my father's for decades), seem to like me. I think this is friendship.

> *Looking back, it wasn't. They did like me. But they weren't about to ask me out to dinner or whatever. I didn't realize this until much later, when I was an adult, and did, actually, become friends with both the Keksts and the Wenders.*

***

I start babysitting for a few families, mostly friends of my parents.

My most regular clients are Justin and Sarah Wender, who are tweens. After a while, they insist that their parents can't go out unless I'm the babysitter. The Wenders live in a very nice apartment near where I live on the upper east side. Ira Wender (their dad) is a lawyer and Phyllis is a literary agent. Justin and Sarah both go to private school.

One night Justin complains about something not being fair. I say "You're right Justin. Life isn't fair. You have two parents who love you, plenty of good food to eat, a warm house to live in and a nice comfortable bed. You are so far ahead on the fairness scale that I don't want to ever hear you complain about that again." I worried a little if I had gone over a line, but I knew their parents pretty well and was pretty sure they would approve, if they heard about it. Justin never complained about fairness again, and he and his sister still wanted me to babysit, so I guess it was OK.

I really like babysitting. Being in charge of something, even for a little while, is a nice change. Being with others who are not my peers and not my age group is wonderful. I like being alone more than most people, but even I have my limits and I regularly surpass them. And the fact that the parents really appreciate me is nice. I mean, the money is fine, but in some ways it's even better to have them ask for me, and say "thank you" and mean it. I'm not sure why the Wender kids insist on me. Maybe I treat them more like adults than other babysitters do. We certainly have some serious conversations, which probably isn't typical of a lot of babysitters.

I also have a small crush on Abby Wender, who is Ira's daughter from an earlier marriage, even though she is five years older than me. It's a weird crush, as I only see her a few times over a few years, but who ever heard of a crush that is rational?

***

I am 15 years old and I see Dad working in the den, which is common. But he's writing lots of numbers. That's unusual.

"Hey Dad, whatcha doing?"

"I'm figuring out how much to pay each partner."

"Based on what?"

"Well, each person gets a share, based on how long they've been a partner and how many hours they bill. But I want to adjust it and if one person's share goes up, other shares have to go down and if one person's share goes down, others have to go up." I use algebra to figure out how to do this so that the gain or loss is spread evenly. He doeesn't understand how i did it, but he can see it works. That's nice. And he's grateful to me, which is also nice.

While I've already found things I know that Dad doesn't, this is the first time I showed him that I knew how to do something mental that he couldn't. I don't understand why he can't figure this out on his own, but he can't. Multiplying with Stern blocks had been cool, but my classmates were little kids and Peggy Stern had understood it as soon as I showed her. This is different. This is Dad. He's a genius, and he had thought about this, and not been able to figure it out. Figuring it out is fun, being smarter than my dad is cool. And weird.

***

In 1975, Rick gets one of the first home computers available. We played Star Trek. Space was a 10x10 field of dots. The Enterprise was an E. The Klingons were K's. It was fun. It was fun playing the game and it was fun being with Rick. He was older than Nancy, and was something like an uncle to me, rather than a brother-in-law.

***

I have one date in high school, with Ottilie, who is probably the smartest girl in my grade. In eighth grade, I invite her to a concert. We sit next to each other. At one point, I put my arm around her shoulder with my hand dangling down and she turns to me and says "*what* are you doing?" That's great. I snatch my hand away and sit in mortified embarrassment for the rest of the concert.

***

Around this time is when Mom first told me about how much she sacrificed for me and how much work Gateway was, and so on. She also notes that she gave up her career as an interior decorator to raise me. I sort of wonder who raised Nancy but guess that she was a latchkey kid, or something.

***

I am 16 years old and Mom tells me I'm going to be an uncle! Nancy is having a baby! This is great news and now there is even *more* reason to visit Chicago. I like all babies, but, from birth, Aaron is an amazingly likable and easy-going child. On each visit I see him not fussing, not doing any of the annoying things that babies can do. His first word is "yes". Aaron likes to master things before he tries them. For a long time, he gets by with only a few words (mommy, daddy, up, yes, no, food, and "ot's dis?" which means "What is this?") Then, one day, full sentences! Aaron likes affection. He will sometimes come up to me and look up and say "Up on Petor!"

One day, when he is 2 years old, he gets upset and tells Nancy: "Mommy, I am very upset. I am going to my room to calm down."

Three years later his brother Jonathan is born. Jonathan is also very likable, but not easy-going. Nancy's nickname for him is "baby doll" and Jonathan calls himself "bee bee da" and soon is frequently saying "be bee da do" which soon changes to "I do by self."

When Jonathan starts preschool at age 3, his big brother sits him down one day and says: "Jonathan, you're going to school now. You should learn to read." Then, in an hour or so, Aaron teaches Jonathan to read.

***

At the end of the year, Mrs. Buglion retires. One day in the hallway, she stopped me and tells me I'm the reason she is quitting. "If kids are going to be like you, I don't want to teach."

***

Tenth grade is simply more of the same, but maybe a little less horrible.

My grades in high school are OK, but nothing to write home about since I never study. Most semesters I'm either just on the honor roll or just off it, which needs an 85 average.

In the spring of 10th grade, the college guidance counsellor (who is the wife of the headmaster) bets me that I can't get a 95 average. I'm pretty sure she just wants to improve the school's record of where kids go to college, but I want the money, so I get a 95 average. Even that doesn't take much work.

Since I have exhausted the math curriculum at York (they don't even offer calculus) it's somehow been arranged for me to take a college computer science class at Hunter College, which I think is cool.

***

It's the first day of the college class. Mom picks me up from York and takes me to Hunter, even though it is less than a mile away and I am 16 years old. Maybe I would have gotten lost a time or two, but I would have found it eventually. We find the room. it's a lecture hall, almost like an auditorium, at Hunter College. There is a big blackboard in the front. The professor walks in. He is a small Asian man and is quite young, not much older than some of the students. He introduces himself in a strong Chinese accent. "My name is professor Ng. But you can't say my name so you call me Professor No Good." I like him right away. Then he says "Anyone want 'A', come to my office, ask me and I give you 'A'". Now everyone likes him!

After that first day, not surprisingly, nearly everyone goes to his office and asks for an "A". I also go to get my automatic A, even though I'm interested in the subject. I mean, I'm not even a real college student yet and this won't be part of my college GPA, but, why not get an A and then concentrate on learning? He seems puzzled that people are taking the class for any reason other than pure interest.

It's a fun class. We learn ALGOL-W and have to submit our programs on punch cards in the basement of one of the buildings. Hunter is so much better than York. There are no adolescents! And I am not the smartest. And I get treated like an adult. And there is a lovely anonymity. There are more kids in that class than in a whole grade at York.

Later in the semester we find out that it's his first semester teaching in America. At another point he tells us that he came to the US by boat and taught himself Polish on the way, just to have something to do.

In the spring semester, I take a math class at Hunter.

Somehow, in 10th grade, I hear about a program called "early admissions" which would let me skip 12th grade and go straight to college. I ask my college guidance teacher about this and read about it in a pamphlet she gets for me. This is for me! A year less of high school! A year less of York!

The pamphlet does note that people who do early admission miss having senior year with your friends, and don't go to their high school graduation or prom. Well, those are the usual downsides but, for me, those aren't bugs, they are features. It's more like "You won't get to be scorned, teased, and bullied for a whole year, and you won't have to ask a girl to go to the prom and get rejected and then spend the evening alone."

Of course I talk about it with Mom and Dad and, separately, with Nancy. They are all on board with it. Nancy, in particular, thinks it would be good for me.

***

The PSATs are given early in the fall semester of 11th grade. I look forward to them. I like standardized tests. I take a couple of practice tests and do fine. I study some words from a book that is supposed to help you get a better score. Other kids seem to dread them or be indifferent.

I take the PSATs with the rest of my class. I do pretty well—650 on both math and verbal, which is 98th and 99th percentile. These are decent scores, but a far cry from double 800s; nonetheless, they are the highest in my grade by 100 points on each test.

And none of the words I studied were on the test.

This is more grist for the teasing mill and the teasing is partly about being 2E, even though no one uses that term. So smart and so stupid is more like it. So I get called both "brainiac" and "retard."

In the spring we take the SATs, right there at York. Since I did fine on the PSATs, I'm not concerned.

As on almost every test I've ever taken, I finish way ahead of time, but they won't let me leave. Teachers have always told me to check my work, but I have tried this and found that, when I check my work, I'm more likely to go from correct to incorrect than vice versa. So, sitting there after the SAT, and not allowed to read a book, I amuse myself by figuring out why the other answers could be correct. That is much more interesting than giving the answer the test writers want!

I get my scores in the mail and I got 680 and 650, again, 99th and 98th percentile. I'm a little disappointed. I know I knew all the answers on the math part, anyway, but I get careless.

Like the WISC all those years ago, the SAT is my salvation. 98th and 99th percentile out of all the people who take the test is way better than an 85 average at York Prep. It's proof that I'm smart, both for me and for other people.

***

Now I have to start looking at colleges. I'm not completely decided about early admissions. Mom and I go to Boston and I really like MIT: I like their nerdy culture, I like their attitude toward sports (they will sponsor and support any intramural team for any sport, but sports are for recreation and they don't compete in NCAA), I love their bookstore, which has a giant poster about the history of mathematics. And it would be nice, if a bit scary, to get away from home.

But my very over-protective mother won't let me leave New York City if I go to college a year early. Getting away from the torture of York and high school seems more urgent than going to MIT (and there's not guarantee I would get in), so I apply to NYU, which is the only place in NYC that offers early admissions.

> *Looking back, I should have investigated schools in Chicago, but I didn't think of it.*

For early admissions students there's an interview. One early fall day, Mom and I head down to NYU on the bus—it's a long ride, but my mom likes the bus. I'm dressed in the same clothes

I wear for York: White buttoned shirt, gray slacks, a blue blazer and a tie. We get off the bus and find the building.

I'm nervous, but not panicky. Maybe Mom is also nervous, I don't know. Does Mom even *get* nervous? I think it will be a long interview designed to weed people out. I show up for the interview. Mom escorts me to the admissions office, naturally, and comes into the interview room, which is an ordinary professor's office with a desk and chairs and so on. The interviewer is a middle-aged man with dark hair. He's sitting on the other side of the desk and Mom and I sit facing him.

"Did you like high school?" I hate high school, but I know that he doesn't want to hear that! So I say "I guess." Then he asks "Do you think you'll like college?" I have no idea whether I will or not, but I say "Sure, I guess."

That's it! That's the whole interview!

About a week later we get a letter. I'm in! I guess that, given my SAT scores, they weren't really interested in my interview. Or maybe it's that my parents will be able to pay the full tuition. Or maybe they just don't budget enough to pay for interviews, I don't know.

It's much easier to survive 11th grade knowing that there won't be 12th.

Chapter 11

Late teens

I've just turned 17. I'm about to start college. It's July 13, 1977. 9:30 PM. I am lying on my bed in my room, where I have lain every night for years. And the lights go out. Not just my light, all the lights. I don't really see a lot of light out my window, even on a normal night, but now it's dark. Really dark. Much darker than normal. Pitch dark.

And I panic a bit. How will I get downstairs in the dark? How do I not fall down the stairs? I decide to crawl, rather than walk, so I can feel ahead with a hand. And I get lost. Never mind falling down the stairs, I can't find the stairs!

This is the same thing that happened back at Gateway with the mask: The world goes away. It's not quite as bad now; I don't start screaming. I'm not crying. I'm worried, but not panicked. I figure out that my parents will find me. But I still get lost in the apartment I've lived in for six years.

I hear my parents calling me, 30 minutes or an hour later. I'm still crawling around near the back door to our apartment. I call back and they find me, with a flashlight. They wonder what I'm doing back there, rather than moving toward the stairs. We all go downstairs, guided by their flashlight. I don't really see their faces, as they are pointing the flashlight away from them.

Turns out the lights went out all over New York City.

***

I am 17 and I am a student at New York University. Mom doesn't think I'll be able to get there by myself. We argue about it, but, while I don't think she wins the argument, she nevertheless finds a college student who's willing to drive me there, wait, and then drive me home. Richard is a nice guy and we sometimes venture out into Greenwich Village to eat at Yonah Schimmel's knishery or wherever. But what the heck do I need a chaperon for? If I get lost, I get lost.

Chaperon issue aside, I love being at a big university. I love slipping through the cracks. I love being in a place where no one knows me, where I can be anonymous. I walk around campus, or down hallways, or into new classes and nothing happens. No teasing. No pointing. No talking. I'm just another kid walking around campus. A bit shorter and thinner and younger than most; somewhat thicker glasses; but nothing special at all. One face and body in a crowd of other faces and bodies.

Even better: NYU doesn't really have a defined campus. The buildings are all in Greenwich Village, in amongst the dorms and the class buildings are all sorts of other buildings—apartment buildings and townhouses and stores and supermarkets. This makes the community even larger and more amorphous, and Greenwich Village is famous for its interesting and quirky character and characters. It is even easier to blend in here than it would have been at some giant university campus.

If I do something dorky in math class or at the chess club, no one else knows about it because each class and club has different people. To be the "odd one" in a school with 120 students does not require much oddness. To stand out at a school with 40,000 students, you really have to be something unusual! In fact, it's safe to say that there is no oddest student at NYU—because there are so many ways to be odd. You could be the tallest or the shortest, you could be the one with double 800s on the SAT (not me!) or the one who had memorized most of The Lord of the Rings and so on and so on. At York, I had the highest SAT scores—not at NYU! At York, I was probably the only one (or one of very few) who didn't care at all about popular culture—not at NYU! At York, I was weird for liking math—Not at NYU!

It's not so much that NYU is "my place" or the ideal school for me. It isn't. I would be more at home at a school like MIT, but they would never have let me in a year early, and might not have let me in at all. NYU is a good school but it is full of a different kind of kid. It's not that NYU is really a party school, but it's not one for nerds and grinds so much, either.

NYU has very few major and minor requirements: Eight courses in your major and four in your minor, over eight semesters. That leaves room for a lot of electives and I love that! There are so many interesting subjects. Sometimes, when I'm sitting in the student center, or before a meeting of a club, or during an all night session of playing games and bullshitting, I hear kids complain that there is nothing they want to take. My mind boggles. They aren't interested in how people think, how societies form, how we lived, how money works, how people are governed or ... *anything*? How is that possible? They aren't stupid. They just aren't interested.

I'm a little older and more mature. More importantly, other people my age are a little older and more mature, too; just as I am now 17 my peers are also 17. And, instead of being among the oldest in my school (being 16 and in my fifth year at York) I am now one of the youngest and newest (17 and a freshman). I was surrounded by adolescents who knew me forever and always viewed me as somewhat alien; now I'm surrounded by young adults who don't know me at all. I start acting like them. I never get into some of the wilder or more raucous activities that my peers do. My one experience with pot terrified me, so I don't do drugs. And, while I do drink, I don't enjoy being drunk, so I don't drink to excess, while most of them do. I've always been risk-averse and that continues as well.

> *In 2007, I read a book called It's so Much Work to Be Your Friend by Richard LaVoie. It says adolescence is about fitting in, while adulthood is about standing out. So, things are getting better.*

There are so many courses to take and things to do! The first semester I sign up for calculus, of course, since I intend to be a math major. I also register for elementary German (a good course for math majors), etymology (fascinating!) and economics I (also fascinating!)

One day I see a sign on a bulletin board for the Science Fiction Club. That sounds cool—I've been reading science fiction fairly obsessively since age 9. Meeting other SF geeks might be fun.

I'm a little nervous, but I go to a meeting in some room at Loeb Student Center, it's just an ordinary room with a big table and a bunch of chairs. I sit in one and no one pays any attention to me, which is a nice change from the negative reactions I would get at York; here, no one knows who I am.

The room is full of people talking about SF; people who are passionate about it. People who, like me, grew up reading Asimov and Heinlein and Clarke, and now read Varley and LeGuin. People who have opinions about all these authors that they are willing, even eager, to share. With anyone. Even me.

When you're weird, finding people with shared interests is vital. In the SF club, people put up with my quirks; they just want to talk about SF (and, let's be frank, SF fans are not without quirks of their own). So I start going to a lot of meetings. But, between meetings, nothing happens.

I've been playing chess for years, so I also join the chess club. This is also a source of quirky people with a niche interest.

***

Unlike a lot of kids who are good at math, I didn't take calculus in high school because York didn't offer it, so I enroll in Calculus 1. The professor is on his last semester of teaching before retirement. He is, to say the least, not very motivated and not at all inspiring. I do OK, getting a B. But a B in a math class is pretty disappointing, and this is just calc 1, which is not even really math, it's more like learning spelling or basic grammar. And I do OK in a weird way. Calculus 1 has some theory elements, such as the epsilon delta proof (you can look it up) that most kids find really hard. And it has applications, which most kids find much easier. I am just the opposite, partly because I have so much trouble visualizing things. Maybe the higher levels of math will be easier, that's sometimes how it works with me.

I discover that I am not quite at good at math as I thought I was. Being the best math student at York Prep isn't really saying much. Other freshman have had far more math than I have and are better at it, as well.

My Calc II professor is a nice enough guy, but he is a very recent immigrant from somewhere in eastern Europe, with his white, button down shirts buttoned up to the neck with no tie; he doesn't speak English very well, and has a very strong accent. I do badly and I stop being a math major. This really sucks. I've always been good at this stuff. If I was *really* good at it, I would have managed to learn calculus, despite the bad professors. But I haven't ever learned to study, and I don't learn how now.

After a semester, Mom figures maybe I can make it there on my own, and I do figure it out. 6 train to Astor Place, then walk two blocks south then turn right and walk until I hit Main Building. But I do sometimes get lost trying to find Courant Institute, where the math courses are, but, when I get lost, I ask for directions. It's not really a problem.

Later I hear that men don't ask for directions. This rule probably existed in the late 1970s, but I am often unaware of these things. This time, that's good.

***

One part of my disability is that I have a lot of trouble taking notes. I've never been good at it. High school was mostly so easy that it didn't matter, especially since I didn't really care if my grades were stellar. Since I never studied, it didn't really matter what my notes were like.

That won't work so well here; I can tell right away that it's a different academic ball game. I figure out that if I do all the readings and go to every class, that's a good start. I'm amazed that many people don't do this. I also figure out that, if I argue with what the professor is saying, I have a much better chance of remembering it. That is, I figure out why what the professor was saying is wrong. Even if I know my argument isn't right, the very act of arguing is a memory aid. This doesn't work so well in math classes, but it works everywhere else.

I learn to distinguish which professors welcome this and which ones don't. This happens the first or second time I ask a probing question. Some professors get into a discussion, or give me references, or ask to talk about it after class. Others react with hostility, some of them seem to be afraid to be challenged, others just don't seem interested. Don't *they* find the subject interesting? Why not? Some students don't ask a single question in a whole semester! What's wrong with them? Aren't the professors interested in the subject? What about the other students?

For the group that doesn't welcome questions, I try to keep the arguing in my head. However, with that first group, once I start arguing, I have trouble stopping.

I mean, at home, arguments just went on and on, so, why not here? In my family, you argue until you win! Mom argues with Dad (but when we bring it up, they say they are "discussing, not arguing"). Jason and I argue with both of them. Where's Macedon (me against Dad)? How do we get home from wherever we are (Dad against Mom)? Should we be required to go to synagogue (Jason, but especially me, against the parents, but mostly Mom)? Is the music too loud (Jason against everyone)? Does it matter if my shirt is tucked in (me and Mom)? How important is grammar (me and Mom)? And so on.

Once, a history professor and I got into a long argument [1] and she said "OK, we are moving on now." I go to the library and find books to show I am right. Not just one, not two, but three books. I bring them in the next time the class meets (I don't remember about what). The professor acknowledges that; she is pretty nice about it. I thank her for acknowledging it; I know enough not to gloat, after all, she's going to give me a grade! But in my head I think "Cool! Right against the professor!"

But after class, several classmates ask why I had done this and I don't know how to respond. I had been right! The professor had been wrong! Who wouldn't bring in books to show that? Turns out, most people wouldn't, but I did. Weird.

> *Decades later, I find out that a lot of neurodiverse people resent having to mask their divergence all their lives. I can understand that it's exhausting, but I wish I had been able to mask. I didn't know what was weird about my behavior and, even if I had known, I don't think I could have masked it.*

Another studying trick is what I came to call super-outlining.

---

[1] I don't remember what it was about.

For a long paper, I make an outline with a lot of levels. It would look something like this:

1. Main topic 1
   a) Subtopic 1.1
      i. Subsubtopic 1.1.1
      ii. Subsubtpic 1.1.2
   b) Subtopic 2.1
      i. Subsubtopic 2.1.1
      ii. Subsubtopic 2.1.2

Only with even more levels and, of course, a lot more items. Then I write a sentence for each level. Then I fix up the grammar and *voila*! I've written the paper.

***

My biggest problem is with German. The professor is nice and reasonably good, but I am just not suited to learning German. I never thought I was great at languages, but I thought I was OK at it. But either that's because the professor's teaching style doesn't match my learning style, or because I am comparing myself to York students, or maybe just because German is hard, despite being relatively close to English, with multiple definite articles and three genders and so on.

***

Freshman year has been pretty good. It's exactly the opposite of York. Academically, it wasn't great. My GPA is 2.425, which is a lot worse than I am used to doing. But outside of academics, everything has changed, and all for the better. I don't exactly have *friends*, whatever they are, but at least I have some agreeable social activities with people who don't shun me.

For my sophomore year I switch to economics. That seems like it has some good math in it, and it's interesting. My intro to economics professor. He's an older guy, Walter Haines [2]. He has white hair and a pale complexion. The class is big, about 60 kids, in a big lecture hall. It's the second or third class he asks "What would happen to the supply of oranges if the price went down? I will bet 50 cents that you can't give the right answer." I say "I don't want to bet but want to try the question" and he says "I tell you what, I will *give* you 50 cents if you are right!" Well, I have no idea about the question! But the obvious answer is that the supply would go down. That can't be it, or he would not have offered the bet. I don't see how it could go up, that makes no sense at all. So I said "no change" and he walks over and gives me two quarters. Cool! I didn't know the subject, but I do know how to take tests. It turns out that, in economics, the supply is a curve. When the price changes, you move on the curve, but the curve stays the same.

But as the class goes on, I discover that the Nobel prize winning economists all disagree with each other about just about everything. That sounds like none of them know what they are talking about. Who wants to study a subject where no one knows what they are talking about? So I drop economics as a major and switch to being a political science major.

I decide I want to live in a dorm for my sophomore year. On a practical level, the commute is a pain in the ass. More importantly, I want to be away from home. Mom gets nervous if I come home late and I don't need that. And being away is one more aspect of growing up. I bring it up with my parents and they are surprisingly OK with it. So, I get a dorm room.

My first roommate is Irving. He is an interesting roommate. For one thing, he is almost never in the room. It turns out that he is almost never in class, either. He has a 0.5 GPA. That takes some effort! He tells me that his parents are divorced and neither

---

[2] I just Googled him. He was born in 1918, so, in 1976, he would have been under 60, I guess that seemed old, but it seems young now!

one wants him to live with them. Yikes! But it's a pretty good transition to a dorm. I'm fine with being alone in my room a lot, and he isn't annoying in any way; he doesn't smoke in the room, he doesn't play loud music, he just sometimes shows up to go to sleep and, once in a great while, talk to me.

In the spring semester I get a triple room with Bob Goldenberg and Michael Edwards-Jones. They are much more congenial and interesting. Michael is from London and his family has lived on the same street for 600 years. His address has no numbers until you get to the post code. Unlike Irving, Bob and Michael are engaging. We do things together in the room and outside. Sometimes we go out to dinner, or we will play a game together. And I'm sort of guessing this is friendship, more or less.

After the spring semester I decide I like living at home better. I have my own room (and it's a lot bigger than the dorm room) and Mom is still cooking meals. But I often get home after dinner. And, even when I was in the dorm, Mom wasn't really absent. She would call the front desk and leave messages reminding me to do my laundry and so on. I never replied to these. If she's going to be bugging me anyway, I might as well eat her meals.

One summer Dad gets me a job as an assistant to several paralegals at Wachtell, Lipton, a rival law firm. Despite popular perception, my dad and the senior lawyer at that firm are friends. We go to their house sometimes, they come to ours. The job is very easy and even I can see that it's sort of a "gimmee" job. But I'm getting paid for hanging out with four attractive young women, so I am definitely not complaining. And they do find some work for me to do.

Anyway, while I'm working there, I hear people say amazing things about my dad. When people hear my name, their reaction is often "You're related to *Joe Flom*!?" My dad is oddly famous; most famous people might be "A list" famous—everyone has heard of them—people like presidents and top athletes and actors. Others might be "C" or "D" list. Their name might be vaguely familiar but you don't know exactly who they are. My dad is "A list" among a certain group and on no list at all among everyone else. I've known this for a long time, certainly since I lay in bed wondering how I could compete with him. But the contrast is still a little jarring.

***

My parents are throwing a party for me. I invite the psychologist who said I would never go to college. To my surprise, he writes back saying he can't attend, but that he was glad he was wrong. I feel proud, too, that I had defied his predictions. Not so much that I've had gone to college—that was always assumed, in my family—but that I've graduated early.

I graduated NYU in February, 1980 at age 20. My GPA isn't great, a little under a B. *Part* of me is adult. I've graduated from college, I did pretty well, I've got the diploma, and I did learn some stuff about specific subjects and about how I learn. But I know I'm really not an adult, not even really a 20 year old. I still am not sure if I have any friends. I lost track of Bob and Michael. I still haven't had sex. After a year in the dorms, I went back to living at home. I don't know *what* I'm going to do for a living. I'm still a weird kid. I'm still broken. I'm pretty sure I will never be whole.

My parents and I drive down to India House, where the party is being held. India House is an old, elegant club in downtown Manhattan. I'm dressed up in a suit. and about 100 people attend, including Jason and Nancy, and Mrs. Friedus and Miss Kumar and Miss Pulanco from Gateway; Mrs. Caushen from Emerson and Dr. Weintrob and Mr. Spaull and Mr. Linton from York; and Rosalinda and Sabha all the way from Ireland and Michael.

Everyone congratulates me, which is kind of embarrassing but kind of nice and I make a short speech, which is fun, and I get presents and stuff.

After graduating, I keep living with my mom and dad. Mom wonders, aloud, why her kids don't move out. I say, "you cook our meals, the cleaning lady cleans up, and you don't charge rent. You didn't raise any morons!" There are other reasons I might have wanted to move out. Mom is domineering and living at home is making it harder for me to grow up, and being around her is a constant reminder, sometimes tacit and sometimes explicit, that I am and was a problem. But, of course, I don't bring those up. Confronting my mother is scary and it seems pointless.

And all this time, I keep visiting Nancy and Rick in Chicago at every opportunity. Their place is still a kind of sanctuary and also a kind of demonstration project, of how people can behave with each other.

Chapter 12

Not quite grown up

It's 1980, I am 21 years old, a recent college grad but still living at home. I'm watching the film *Ordinary People* and, as I watch, the Beth Jarrett character (played by Mary Tyler Moore), is reminding me more and more of my mother. Beth is a wealthy woman with two sons. The older son dies in a boating accident caused by the younger one, who then is hospitalized with severe PTSD and later attempts suicide. Beth, like my mom, is a wealthy, white woman with two sons and a rather cold relationship with her husband.

The particulars are mostly different. No kid in my family died (although I sometimes joke that two other Flom kids died in infancy because their egos got crushed out of existence). No one in my family has PTSD. No one has been hospitalized. But, as I watch, I realize that what is wrong with Beth is similar to what is wrong with Mom. She wants things to look good, and is less concerned with whether they actually *are* good. Mom wants me to be "normal" not so much because I would be happier, but because it would reflect better on her. I don't think she even recognizes that I'm miserable, that I have been miserable for a long time, that I am angry a lot of the time, that I feel broken, and that I am still sure I will never be whole. She doesn't know any of that.

But she knows I am weird. She knows *that*! She started Gateway because I was weird, she writes the checks for therapy, she has seen me come home from school way late after detention, with my shirt half-tucked in, and my tie askew. She is always trying to fix my clothes, or get me to do it. To no avail. But she's never asked why I come home late from school. Maybe she just figured I was doing some proper thing such as being in a club or hanging out with friends. Or maybe she didn't want to know.

Why does she think I've been in therapy for so long? Because I'm *happy*? Because of my great relationship with her? Because of my relationships with other people? I'm not in therapy because I am weird. I'm in therapy because I am miserable. She doesn't see. All this last 20 years, I could have dealt with a messy house and some badly cooked meals, but if I could have had a mother who saw me, that would have been good. Dad doesn't seem to see me either, but he is never home.

My mother sees (but fails to see) me, she sees a person to be fixed, a mirror that distorts her own image; she remembers Nancy; I am not Nancy. Nancy, from everything I know, had a relatively normal childhood and adolescence. Of course, to me, she was hardly a normal anything: She was Nancy! She had friends, she liked music, she did OK in a relatively normal school, she went to a normal college and did reasonably well, she had boyfriends and then fell in love and got married and had kids and all the normal things.

My mother sees (but fails to see) Jason. She sees that he is engaged in typical activities for his age, like sports and music, she sees that he goes to friends' houses and invites them to ours, she sees that he has girlfriends, she does not see that he is drinking and doing drugs. How has she not smelled pot in his room for years? How does she not know that he is cheating his way through high school? Even that behavior of Jason's is normal, albeit in a negative way. A teenager drinking and doing drugs? What are the odds?

I tried pot once, when our parents were away. I had a psychedelic, out-of-body experience and did not enjoy it at all. It was scary. It was out of control, and that scared me. When I described it to my brother he said that that is what he is like when he drops acid.

My mother knows I am not normal. All those *What to Expect* books came out long after I did, but I would not have matched any of it. She never tells me "I hate you because you're not normal!" or anything like that, but I can sense it. I think I may have absorbed it with mother's milk, I certainly don't remember when it started. Part of it is that she has told me, more than once, how much she gave up to raise me, how she started Gateway and was devoted to it, and so on. She never explicitly says "why aren't you more like your brother?" but the way she reacts to him and to me implies it. This is implicit in her telling me about giving up a career, in telling me how much trouble I was to raise, from birth.

What to Expect When Your Child is 20 never gets written, but I wouldn't match that, either. Your 20 year old should be in college or working. Nope. Your 20 year old likely has had romantic relationships. Nope. Your 20 year old has several friends. Nope. None of that. Even my hobbies are a bit off. I don't play baseball, I play chess. I don't collect coins, I (briefly) collected political buttons, back in my teens. I also briefly had a collection of fliers from whorehouses that I got on the streets when I was a teen. I just thought it was amusing that they were handing these out to a kid who was underage and looked even more underage.

Mom spends so much of her time trying to be, not normal, but a kind of uber-normal, a perfect mother. I never make my bed (I never figure out how). Most people do, but she not only makes beds, she strips them down to the mattress each morning and then remakes them from scratch. (She has always done this for her own bed; when Jason and I were kids, we were in charge of our own bed making, but at Beechwood, she does it for ours too.)

Many mothers make dinner for their families, mine makes multiple course dinners for us every night, even when she is going out. She's been doing this as far back as I remember, although I did start doing some cooking in my teens. Other families sometimes order in, we don't. Other houses are sometimes messy (or so I hear), but ours is not: There is never a dish or a pot left in the sink.

Mom is always worrying about what others think of her, and she is always worrying what they are thinking of me, and that it wasn't good. I envision her thinking that her friends wonder why her son is so weird and what is wrong with her that produced such a child. I use this against her; when she complains about me, I will tell her "well Mom, you are half the nature and more than half the nurture, so ...".

When I leave the movie, I am pretty sure that none of this will change my relationship with Mom right away. It's more of a seed, growing, letting me see her in a new light and with new eyes. More grown up eyes. More open eyes.

***

I am 20 years old and, all my life, people have been telling me I ought to go to law school and that I would make a good lawyer. So, I apply to a few law schools and get into Fordham.

At orientation, all of us are sitting in a big auditorium, thinking we know what to expect and that this will be kind of boring but necessary. A few people are sitting on the stage. I'm a little worried, everyone says law school is a lot of work, but I'm not worried about orientation.

The dean stands up and goes to the lectern in the center of the stage. He says:

> Some of you are here because you want to be lawyers. Some of you are here because your parents want you to be lawyers. And some of you are here because you're good at school and don't know what else to do.

I'm in that third group, and I realize that that is not a good thing; I wonder if I'm making a big mistake. I like the classes and

I like my professors and I seem to be keeping up. I do terrible on mid-terms and this really upsets me. I've hardly ever done badly at school and most of those times I was either trying to do badly (e.g. that Spanish class at York) or there was an obvious reason (my calculus 2 professor). This time, neither applies. I don't know what I'm doing wrong.

After midterms, my criminal law professor asks to see me. Fordham has two criminal law professors. Mine is Maria Marcus. She is a small, middle-aged blond woman. Sitting in her office, she tells me she was surprised I had not done well on the exam because I did well in class.

"Which study group are you in?"

"What are study groups?"

She looks shocked.

She explains that most law school students join study groups to help each other and to divide up the work and so on. I didn't even know there were any. This feels even worse than doing badly. Lots of kids do badly in law school, it's notoriously hard and it's notoriously hard even for kids who did well in earlier school. I don't like failing, but it's normal. But her reaction tells me that I have, once again, missed something big. That's weird.

Other students figured out there were study groups in the first days of school, they got asked to join, or they started their own. They may even have chosen among several. I was clueless. I did hang out with some other students to eat and whatnot, some of them, at least, must have known about study groups. But no one let me know. I bet they all assumed I was in one, or had turned them down.

I enrol for the second semester, but do something between dropping out and flunking out. I go to class but don't study. I've told my parents my grades, but I don't want to tell them I am quitting. I duly get a lot of bad grades and that's it for law school.

***

I am 21, working at Kekst & Co., a public relations firm where I had had a summer job a couple years earlier. After the law school fiasco, I ask for and get a full time job there in the summer of 1981. It's a relatively small firm in an office building in midtown Manhattan. Gershon Kekst is the founder and head of the firm; he is a client and friend of my dad's, and I like him too.

But I am not happy at all at Kekst. I don't like corporate life; it isn't so much Kekst & Co. itself (and Gershon Kekst, who started the firm, is excellent) but I don't want to work for a for profit. Helping companies make themselves look good offends my liberal sensibilities; I am aware that I have been enormously lucky in life and want to give back. But, beyond that, office work like this just doesn't sit well with my 2E and my LD. I don't know exactly why.

> *Looking back, Kekst (and corporate life generally) is very hierarchical. Gershon was at the top, then partners, then associates (like me) then secretaries and then mail room staff and so on. I knew that at the time. But there was relatively little mixing. People were mostly polite to people at other levels, but they didn't really interact. My closest relationships are with the senior partner, one associate, one intern, and one guy in the mail room. I didn't know this was wrong, I didn't even recognize that there was a rule about this.*

Mostly, I write short things for annual reports and so on and that goes OK. But then I write one big paper and it comes back from Gershon with a note on one of those tiny post-its: "Fix this." There's nothing else! I'm used to professors who will write lots of notes, even (or especially) if they don't like something. I don't know what to do. I go and show it to Dad and ask him what the note means and he says "That is an excellent note. It means you should fix this."

***

I am 22 years old and visiting my sister in Chicago. Some friends of theirs come over and they have a young daughter, maybe 3 years old. Naturally, I play with her. Little kids are fascinating and are so much easier than older kids or adults. They tell you what they want, they tell you what they think, and they are eager to be friends. All you have to do is listen. And play.

Before I know it, it is time for them to leave. A couple of hours have gone by. The parents tell me no one had ever entertained their daughter so well. That feels good, but I can't really figure out why the girl would have been hard to entertain.

Later, before dinner, Nancy and I are talking and she tells me that the kid is autistic and I realize she had been a bit odd. While we were playing, we were just playing and she was just a little girl.

I've always liked kids, but maybe I'm especially good at kids with issues?

***

A few months later, while still working at Kekst, I hear about Ramapo Anchorage Camp in Rhinebeck, NY. They are a camp for kids with all sorts of issue from age 4 to 18. I apply to be a counsellor, even though I am kind of old for the job at 23. I get the job! That's exciting. It seems like a good opportunity. Law school wasn't for me, neither was corporate life. And even though I hated my own camp experience, being a counsellor at a place like Ramapo seems like it could be a better fit. Some of the kids are like I was. The camp is designed for them — for me. It seems likely to be less hierarchical, and it's definitely a way of giving something back. And I might even be good at it.

I talk about it with Mom and Nancy and they are encouraging—naturally, Nancy is both more encouraging and more engaged with my decision.

When summer rolls around, I take the train up to Rhinebeck and get shown around the camp. There are two areas with cabins, separated by a path that is about 1/4 mile long and that goes up a hill. There is a lake for swimming and boating; there are areas for different activities and crafts and sports, all typical camp stuff. But the stalls in the bathrooms in the cabins have doors that don't lock, because some kids will lock themselves in and not come out and some will hurt themselves in the toilets. That's OK with me. I'm not modest in that way at all. I do wonder about some of the female counsellors. Not surprisingly, there are more female counsellors than male ones, and more male campers than female ones. None of the girl counsellors have to sleep in boys bunks, but they do spend most of their time with them. But no one leaves.

This is clearly camp, so it has something in common with the places I went. It's in the woods. It has similar activities. The cabins are cabins and the beds are simple frame beds and so on. But it's also different. The other counselors are very welcoming; many have been counselors here for years and years, others are new. But we are all in it together.

We arrive several days before the campers. We all learn about where we will be assigned and sleeping. There is a long weekend of training for us counsellors. One speaker is a psychologist who specializes in treating kids with issues. One young female counselor asks "What if I do something that makes it worse?" The psychologist replies "You're not here for the hours, because they are longer here. You're not here for the parties, 'cause there are better parties other places. You're here because you love kids. They'll know."

We also learn about how to restrain a kid without hurting them, and that we should always call for help if in any doubt (it is very hard to restrain another person, even if they are much smaller than you are). The craft counsellors learn about other kinds of emergencies. I am going to be an education counsellor—basically a tutor—for a bunch of kids. I will help them with whatever they are struggling with. I'm also a bunk counsellor.

We have something like three evenings off every 2 weeks, which we all use to take a bus into town and do laundry (no one trusts the camp laundry) and eat and drink. The bus driver tells us "I leave on time. If I see you running toward the bus, I still leave on time." When we're at camp, we're on duty, even if we aren't working. We're on duty even when we are sleeping.

It's a lot of work but a lot of fun. Even with all the work, there's some socializing. I see some romantic partnerships develop. There's one woman I like. Her name is Louise. She has dark curly hair (not as curly as mine) and is about as tall as me. She's a little older than most of the counsellors, around my age, which is attractive. I ask her "out" but she very nicely tells me that she prefers girls. Then she is upset about telling me and I say "It's OK. I made a pass and it was intercepted." But, per usual for me, I don't make any real friends.

One month my bunk consists of severely disabled adolescent boys. There's Neil, who wakes up every morning and says, "How many days until visiting day? It's not this Sunday, it's not next Sunday, it's the Sunday after that." He gradually counts down.

The day after visiting day, we're all looking forward to silence but no. Neil wakes up and, again asking and answering his own question: "What day do we go home? It's not this Sunday, it's not next Sunday, it's the Sunday after that." Another countdown begins. This doesn't seem to reflect any misery at camp, it's just something he has to do. I get it, I think. The world is confusing and Neil is seeking order.

There's Fred, a very sweet 15 year old boy who spends every minute he can swinging on the kids' swings and who is terrified of his socks. Some counsellors try to discourage him from swinging but I figure he needs it. Maybe it's even a kind of meditation. When he swings, he looks completely relaxed, while ordinarily he seems a little worried, although it is hard to tell.

Bradley is a compulsive liar.

"My father owns the New York Yankees!"

"No he doesn't, Bradley. George Steinbrenner owns the Yankees."

"I mean he owns the Mets!"

Bradley insists, repeatedly, that he is perfectly normal and doesn't belong in this bunk. Typically, he says this while running around the bunk and flapping his arms.

Mark wets the bed every night, no matter how often we wake him up; when a 6 foot tall kid wets the bed, it gets really wet. We counsellors change the sheets each morning. Luckily, the mattresses are designed for bed wetters and aren't absorbent.

Then there's Joe, a rather round boy, who introduces himself with "I'm Joe Katz!" even if he's seen you earlier that day and who, on encountering any difficulty, lies flat on the ground and says "That's it! I quit! I've had enough!" Whereupon one of us will talk to him a bit and encourage him and, soon enough, he is on his feet again.

An interesting bunch.

One kid can tell you the exact time of day, any time, even if you wake him in the middle of the night, but can't tell time. Another doesn't feel pain. At all. This is really dangerous. Once (not at camp) he broke his leg and didn't notice. And yet, he's ticklish.

I loved that first summer and decide to do it again next year.

It's June and I am part of what is called "mild month" which is for 4 to 6 year old kids (yes, sleep away camp for kids that age) from very troubled homes. One little kid wakes up early each morning and stands next to his clothes, jumping up and down and saying "I'm cold! I'm cold!" Two little girls arrive with only the clothes on their backs and a toothbrush for each. Once, a kid wakes me up by peeing on me.

There's a weird mix of emotions from all this. Of course, the kids are very cute. Regardless of anything else, they are 4 and

5 year old children and are naturally adorable. And there's pity, because they are so damaged so young, born into horrible situations and just trying to make the best of it. And there's sadness because, as much as we can do in the month, then they have to go back to the same situations. But there's also pride and joy. I'm pretty good at this. I tolerate the bad stuff better than a lot of people and I find joy in their small progress. But, then, there's also hope. I was messed up as a little kid, too. True, I was messed up in very different ways from these kids, but I was messed up. And now I'm doing this.

Maybe I'll never be whole. But maybe I am more than whole. And maybe they will, too.

Those are two great summers.

Something else that happens at Ramapo is that I start disclosing that I'm learning disabled. I disclose a lot and I disclose inappropriately. When we counsellors are relaxing in the evening, chatting rather aimlessly, I will just tell people I am learning disabled. And, when I disclose, I want not just sympathy but complete accommodation. I don't always explicitly tell people what I want, and I never say I want it because I am LD, but I want it. I want them to know what to do. Even though I am older than most of the counsellors, in some ways, I'm more like a camper.

This is one stage on the route to accepting myself—I think there are four stages of acceptance of any disability:

Denial *There's nothing wrong with me. There must be something wrong with you!*

Depression *There's something wrong with me. Life stinks.*

Demand *There's something wrong with me. You deal with it.*

Dealing *There's something wrong with me. I better deal with it.*

For much more on these stages see Appendix B on 206

***

Many of the counsellors (including me) know how to juggle. Juggling has a bunch of advantages for special ed kids (and adults). It's noncompetitive (and many of these kids lose at competitions). You can practice alone (so it's not embarrassing). It doesn't involve teams (so you don't have teammates to get mad at you).

So, we teach the kids (and other counsellors) to juggle. This has amazing effects. Some people learn quickly and some take a long time. One counsellor is doing a three ball cascade (the most basic juggle) after a few minutes; he's an athlete and a musician and just generally physically skilled. Learning has the biggest impact on the kids who take a long time, because these kids are not good at physical activities, including sports. And they've been told that. And now, suddenly, they can do something their classmates can't do.

So. During free time some of the counsellors will juggle and some of the kids will want to do so. We give each of them a ball or beanbag and tell them "toss it from one hand to another. Toss it so that it goes as high as your eyes." They do that. Some of them do it well the first time, some need practice. Campers divide among counsellors.

"Now toss it back. Try to only watch it at the peak. Do that a lot. Do it until it's automatic."

And the kids do it! Over and over. When they get that (either in a few minutes, or many minutes, or even another night), we continue. We give them another ball or beanbag. "Put one in each hand. Toss, toss. Start with your worse hand. Toss, toss." And the kid would do it.

"Now, try alternating hands that you start with. Toss left to right, then right to left, then fake a toss from left to right. Then right to left. Keep going." And the kid would do it. Then ... three balls! Toss, toss, toss! And they are juggling! And the kid's face would light up and they would practice. And my face would light up too. Not only are they juggling, but they are learning about practicing.

One thing I like about teaching juggling is that it's not about the teacher. The teaching is easy, certainly for the basic juggle. Another thing I like about teaching juggling to special needs kids (or adults) is that the rewards are so great.

***

As I ride the train home after my second summer at Ramapo, I'm thinking that I'm good with these special needs kids. Playing with the little girl in Nancy's apartment had been one sign. My two summers experience at Ramapo had confirmed it. I start thinking about pursuing a master's in special education with the intention of eventually teaching special ed preschool.

I talk to lots of people about this: My parents, Nancy, and so on. Most people encourage me. I decide to ask Elizabeth Freidus, who had started Gateway with my mom, what she thinks about it. She knows me best, at least in terms of my disabilities; and she knows far more about education than anyone else I talk to. And she is willing to tell me bad stuff, which very few people are.

She tells me it's a bad idea. She even knows *where* my problem will be: "Teachers deal with groups of kids, not individual kids. Everyone has trouble handling groups of kids, but I think it will be especially hard for you. I'm not sure you'll be able to learn it."

But I ignore her and enroll at NYU to get a Master's in early childhood special education. The course work is no problem at all, I mostly get A's. But I am awful at student teaching. At Ramapo-Anchorage and in my other dealings with kids, it had been one-on-one. Teaching is not. You have to keep track of all the different kids and you have to read the body language and voices of all the different kids. These are exactly the sorts of things I can't do.

***

Another thing I can't do, as I've said, is art. But if you tell professors and students of special education that you can't draw, it's like waving a red flag in front of a bull. They can teach me! Everyone can learn to draw! No. I can't. There are others who cannot. Not only is this very frustrating, it's also worrying, because it shows that, even in people who are studying special ed., there's this myth that everyone can learn everything and an unwillingness to accept that some people can't, but that that's okay. It would be much healthier to teach kids that it's not the end of the world to not be able to do something rather than to insist that they can learn. And I would have thought that, if anyone would understand this, it would be special ed teachers. But it isn't.

***

One morning, I am teaching "circle time", with a class of 10 preschoolers sitting in a circle and talking about all sorts of things. One kid jumps up and runs into the hall. I haven't managed to settle the others down, either. I can't manage them and then I'm out in the hall chasing and screaming at the kid who has escaped and even after I catch him (it took me a while, even though he is a little kid) I don't know what to do, because the other kids are still inside and the whole morning gets shot to hell while the other teachers try to restore some sort of normalcy to the day. I feel horrible. In the moment I was panicked and I am still totally frustrated and upset.

Later, the other teachers try to be nice to me in analyzing what went wrong, but they don't figure out what I am missing. Elizabeth did get it. I don't get all the little cues that people (and especially kids) give off all the time, telling a perceptive person what to do. Good teachers are better than average at reading these. I am much worse. There's also my problem with peripheral vision—one problem with seeing out of only one eye at a time is that my peripheral vision stinks.

That's the worst of the teaching experiences, but it's not atypical.

The kids aren't the only problem. At one placement, during an orientation meeting in the classroom, I say to the other staff (who will be supervising me) "Please tell me in words what I was doing right and wrong, because I didn't get body language and stuff." They say they will do that. But, as I will soon learn, they don't.

That semester goes very badly and I get dismissed midway through it. I ask why, and they say "We've been showing you why all semester!" But they did it with body language and other nonverbal cues. So, even in a special ed environment, people don't get it when I explain my issues. This really sucks. No one gets me. If anyone would, it's them, and they don't.

Elizabeth was right I'm not going to be a special ed teacher, or, really, any kind of teacher. That dream lasted a couple years before it died. At least it wasn't a very long-lived dream; and I still do know that I'm good with kids, just not groups of them.

Chapter 13

Israel

I am 25 years old and our family is on vacation in Israel, along with the Caiola family who are all friends of ours. Israel is great! I like it a lot more than I have liked any other place we've visited, like Rome or Spain or Scotland.

It's not so much the famous stuff, the touristy stuff. Sure, that stuff is great. But that's for tourists. What really appeals to me is the people. Many characteristics of Israelis that other people find problematic, I find delightful. They are pushy. Me too. They can be rude. Me too. They tell you exactly what they think. Me too. And they have very little tolerance for bullshit. Me too.

After two great weeks, we come home, I start thinking about moving there, but I am a little skeptical. I was a tourist. I know that's not the same as living there.

There is even an Israeli joke about this. One night, David Ben-Gurion (who was prime minister of Israel) has a dream that he is dead. God talks to him.

"You're David Ben-Gurion! What can I do for you?" "Let me see what heaven is like." And he sees everyone standing around on clouds, doing nothing, very boring. So then he says "OK, now let me see hell." And hell is great! Lots of eating and drinking, people talking and arguing, music playing and so on. In the morning he wakes up. Then, a few months later, he dies and, just like in his dream, God asks what he wants. "I want hell." "You're sure? You want hell?" and he says "yes." Hell is awful! Hot, humid, working all day and night, nothing to eat. He goes to God to complain. "Hey! When I saw this in a dream, it was great! What's going on?" And God says: "*Then* you were a tourist. *Now* you live here!"

I had been a tourist. Do I want to live there?

One advantage would be being 5,000 miles away from my parents. I would cut the apron strings big time. Mom won't even be able to reach me easily by phone, since phone lines are hard to get. My mother is not going to be easy to get away from, but this will do it.

And I need to do it. I don't really know why I need to, but I know I do. I need to be *away*. I need to be alone. I need to be in a place where I am in charge of me. I need to be where I can screw up and have it hurt me. I need to be a grown up. This isn't some sudden realization. It was part of the reason I moved to a dorm for two semesters; it was even part of the reason I thought about moving in with Nancy. I know there are adults who live with their parents, but I can't do that.

But one problem with being 5,000 miles away from Mom is that I'm 6,000 miles away from Nancy—maybe I even need that.

But do I want to live there?

My parents have a good friend (Jo) who is Israeli, and he has an employee (Mickey) who has an empty room in Tel Aviv, so, I move in for a bit. It's even better that Mickey's work keeps him busy all the time and often away. I don't want to be entertained. I want to see what Israel is like.

So, I spend a few weeks, just trying to get a feel for the place. I shop for myself, I cook, I go out for meals sometimes. I do laundry. I pretend I'm Israeli. Of course, unlike most Israelis, I don't have a job so I have a lot of idle time. I sit in cafes or in parks and observe.

After those weeks, I still like it! I don't call home much. And I'm not homesick. I like Israelis. I like the culture, with its emphasis on children. I like the connectedness of people; Israel is the size of New Jersey and has the population of Brooklyn. Not everyone knows everyone, but everyone has connections. If you meet one person, you meet a whole bunch of people because you meet all their connections; that's true everywhere. But in Israel, the web is much tighter.

I like Tel Aviv. It's a modern city with good public transit (although no subways). It's laid out very much on a north-south orientation, running along the Mediterranean. I hear a saying: "Jerusalem studies, Haifa works, Tel Aviv parties." I am not a big partier, and it's a long time before I visit Haifa, but this does seem to fit.

It's a much smaller city than New York, but it has all the things associated with cities: Lots of restaurants, museums, concert halls, lots of different neighborhoods, and so on. As for climate, if you think of Southern California, you won't be far off: Hot dry summers and cool damp winters (but no earthquakes!)

I decide to move there; more, I decide to make aliyah, which means becoming an Israeli citizen. I decide to tell my parents right away, rather than waiting until I am back in the States. It will be easier over the phone. But I'm not all that nervous.

I call my parents to tell them. Mom answers and it is one of the very few times my mother was speechless. There was just silence over the phone line. But how can she object? Her son wants to move to Israel! No Jewish mom could object to that. After a pause she manages to say something noncommittal. Cool. I'm doing this. And I'm doing it regardless of what they say, even though they don't say anything negative. I get tickets home.

I'm excited to be moving. But it will take a while because there is a lot to arrange. Since I want to be an oleh chadash (new immigrant; rhymes with go the ha mosh), I have to apply to make aliyah (emigrate). Of course that involves a bureaucracy and takes time. I will be moving to a maon olim (dormitory for new residents) in Ramat Aviv (a very near suburb of Tel Aviv, almost more like a neighborhood). I have to pack, but the packing is relatively minimal as there is not much space in the room. And I enroll in an introductory Hebrew class at the World Zionist Organization.

I try to do everything as quickly as possible, because, now that I have made the decision, I want to do it. At the Hebrew class I learn that many people take years to move after having made the decision. Of course, it's easier for me, as a single person, than it would be for a family, but still, it seem that a lot of people take a very long time. Not me!

At a maon olim you pay minimal rent for a sort of dormitory room, but a little more spacious and with a kitchen and a bathroom. These are places for adults to live while they adjust to Israel, rather than places for students to live for a few months at a time. Single people share rooms.

Finally it's all arranged. It's June, 1985. I get a one way plane ticket to Tel Aviv.

After the long flight, I take a car to the maon with my bag (other stuff was shipped). When I move in, my roommate is away, so I put my stuff away in what is clearly going to be my half of the room. The room isn't too bad, but some genius has designed the building so that all the windows face south. The west coast of Israel is pretty hot and, in summer, it is very sunny. And there is no space for an AC.

After a few weeks of sweating, and learning more Hebrew, and getting to know Tel Aviv a little better, my roommate comes back. Dov Pollack is a nice guy, we become friends. Lucky for me, Dov is a big extrovert and knows lots of people. Back in the states he was a therapist but now he works as an extra in movies. He introduces me to some other people; we both become good friends with Josef, who is an engineer from Turkey. Although I am 26, moving to Israel makes me feel fully adult for the first time. There is no phone in our room. Mom can only leave messages with the front desk. And she does. She reminds me to do my laundry. But I can safely ignore her. She is thousands of miles away and cannot tell if my clothes are clean or not. It's up to me to decide if they are clean enough. It's up to me to shop for food and cook it. This feels good. This feels liberating. This feels adult.

And now that I'm an adult, hanging out with adults is not so odd. Even though Dov is a quite a bit older than I am, now it doesn't matter, we are both adults.

Many weekends, the three of us go for drives in Josef's car (a BMW). Josef tells us that if he is ever stopped for speeding he starts babbling to the police in Turkish. Many cops know English, or Arabic, but Turkish? They let him go rather than try to hunt down a police officer who speaks Turkish. On some trips, we visit tourist sites, such as kochav ha Yarden, which is a Crusader fortress overlooking the Jordan River. The fortress is amazingly well preserved and the Jordan is amazingly narrow. You could practically jump across.

Is this what friendship is?

My parents' friend Jo Elmaleh and his parents introduce me to some people, notably Rachel and Mordechai (Motka) Limon. Motka was one of the heroes of the war for Israeli independence back in 1948. His wife Rachel is a woman after my mother's heart—a wonderful cook and the sort of homemaker who irons the underwear (I don't think even my mother does that!) They are my parents generation. Motka was born in Poland but grew up in Tel Aviv before Israel was a country. Rachel used to work for the World Zionist Organization. Motka is a big, solid man. Despite smoking a lot and drinking a lot and being quite overweight, he swims a mile or two every day in the Mediterranean (unless there's a thunderstorm) and can carry multiple cases of wine up two flights of stairs. Rachel is a pretty and vivacious middle aged woman with dark hair. They have a daughter a little older than me who is married to a Rothschild, their house is generous but by no means a mansion (flaunting your wealth is not an Israeli thing).

***

Most Israelis speak some English; nearly all the Israelis I interact with regularly speak English pretty well. But, the language of Israel is Hebrew. That's what people speak to each other all the time. Nearly every Israeli speaks Hebrew (even if they speak some other language at home). Since I want to live in Israel and be an Israeli, I start taking Hebrew classes as soon as I arrive. Sure, it's possible to live in Israel and speak only English. Many do. But I am 26 years old, I'm just getting started on adulthood, I want to be as Israeli as I can be. This place makes me happy. This place makes me grown-up. I plan to live in Israel for 50 years or so. I don't want to live like a tourist. That would be fine if I was a retiree or something, but I'm not. And, even though my friends and colleagues all speak English, I don't want to impose on them. Nor do I want to limit myself. And some Israelis speak English very badly, or not at all.

Israel provides cheap Hebrew classes in what is known as an ulpan (rhymes with fool Don). Class meets for a few hours a day, several times a week. All they do is teach Hebrew.

As the weeks go by, I do pretty well, not great, but okay, with the oral language, although I have a very thick American accent. Speaking is easier than listening because, if I don't know a word, I can usually make up some alternative, but if I don't know a word that someone else says, I miss the meaning. I start getting creative with it.

One assignment in class is to write about our dream house. Most people write pretty boring pieces. Huge mansions, swimming pools, that sort of thing. Hebrew has a case system, including a reflexive case, so I make up a house that will "clean itself" by inventing a reflexive form of "to clean." My house will also "make itself bigger" when guests come over.

I have a harder time with reading and an even harder time with writing.

My handwriting is awful and learning a whole new alphabet is really hard. This sucks, but, since my handwriting is so bad, I'm used to not writing by hand. And, fortunately, I really don't have to read or write much. I do speak a lot. I make myself talk each day until I have made 10 mistakes that I recognize. Often, this means I talk to myself, so I will narrate my activities to myself, saying things like "Now I am walking on Dizengoff Street". After about a year of classes and practicing, I am able to make myself understood pretty well and understand most conversations.

I love Israel, but, wherever I am, I have a lot of problems with the nonverbal aspects of communication. These problems are both worse and better in a new country. They are worse because I have to learn new codes of nonverbal conduct. Israelis stand closer to each other than Americans. Gestures are different (for instance, if you hold your hand up, with the palm facing you and your thumb against your other fingers, it means "hold on" or "just a minute". In America, this is often a rude gesture). Israelis touch more. I'm not a toucher. But they are better because, fortunately for me, one of the differences is that Israelis are very direct, and that suits me fine. For instance, if you ask someone a question they may simply say "No" where Americans would give an excuse, so I don't have to interpret what people are saying.

Still, the differences, and my failure to adapt to them, are a problem in assimilating to Israeli society, just as they have been a problem for me assimilating into American society. Just like natives, immigrants pick these things up wherever they are living, but I don't. In Israel, I have the excuse of being foreign. That doesn't really make it easier, but it does let people think "oh, Peter's strange, he's American." But I'm a foreigner in my own land, as well.

***

It's still the summer that I moved to Israel, I'm lying, sweating, in my room, and there's a knock on the door. It's a man I don't recognize, although I fail to recognize many people who I know. "Greetings from Gershon!" he says (Gershon was my boss at a job I had in New York). I relax a little; I really don't know him. He introduces himself as Aryeh (Arik) Carmon.

I let him in and we talk.

PETER: So, how do you know Gershon?
ARIK: I'm the CEO of the Israel-Diaspora Institute. We work to get Diaspora Jews involved in Israel in more ways than just writing checks. Gershon is a big supporter.
PETER: That's interesting.
ARIK: Did you know that the Knesset was only formed to write a constitution? And they haven't managed it yet. So, we are looking for constitutional experts to help us wrote one.
PETER: I didn't know that. There are certainly a lot of Diaspora Jews who are lawyers!
ARIK: Would you like to come work for us?
PETER: What do you want me to do?
ARIK: We need someone to help with research, and writing, and editing, and other things. Gershon told me I should hire you.
PETER: [*I haven't really been looking for a job. I know I will get one eventually, but I want to get better at Hebrew first. But this is close to an ideal job for me.*] Sounds good to me!

The IDI is a tiny group with just three employees (I am number 4). On my first day I get introduced to everyone (that takes 5 minutes). Shelly is from England and Sheila (yes, of the three employees, one is Shelly and one is Sheila) is from South Africa. Then I start work, doing whatever Arik wants (and, to some extent, what Shelly or Sheila want). Both of them are very welcoming. I help organize their computer (none of them are tech savvy), I help Arik find the right words in English (his English is very good, but he learned a lot of it while getting his history PhD at the University of Wisconsin, and it shows, he tend to use fancier words than are really needed, and to write complex sentences where simple ones would do) and just doing whatever.

IDI is a good place to work. I get to wear shorts to work and Arik is a great boss, very gemutlich [1]. Very soon after I start work, he introduces me to his family (his wife Tzipa and their two little kids) and often invites me over for a meal at his apartment. It's a nice place with a bunch of plants in pots and a big floor to ceiling window. Tzipa is a very attractive woman in her 30's; she has dark hair and eyes.

Today at work, I hear Arik ask Sheila to call Tzipa at work (she is a corporate executive) and pass the phone to him. Then I hear him say "Tzipush! Tzipush! Do you know how lucky I am that you married me?" I am amazed. He called his wife at work for no particular reason, no emergency, but just to say he loves her? Is *this* how normal couples behave? I've never heard my mother say "I love you" to my dad, much less call him at work to tell him that she does!

It's February 10, 1986, my first Mother's Day in Israel. Arik invites me over to celebrate with them. Soon after I arrive their three year old son, who doesn't speak any English yet, turns to Tzipa and says (in English) "Mommy, I love you so mush!" Tzipa sort of loses it at this point and starts crying and hugging her husband and their son. I keep my reaction to myself, but I'm amazed again. It must have taken Arik hours, spread out over weeks, to teach the child to do that! And Arik knew how it would affect her, too, much more than any physical gift.

As I watch all this, I'm thinking that I never heard any of that sort of thing between my parents. Emotions such as love and affection were not expressed and such reactions did not happen. In fact, once, when Dad got Mom a Mother's Day gift, she got mad at him and said "I'm not your mother!" I know my parents' ways

---

[1] "Gemutlich" is a Yiddish word meaning, literally "cosy" but it connotes an easiness and comfort

of being with each other are pretty distant, but I don't know if Arik and Tzipa are typical or at some other extreme. I don't have much experience seeing couples interact, but Nancy and Rick are intermediate between my parents and the Carmons. Nancy never did anything like what Arik did, but she was affectionate toward Rick. They would get each other thoughtful gifts and express their fondness for each other in all sorts of ways.

***

I've been in Israel for about a year and I move out of the maon and into my own apartment. It's a one bedroom, a third floor walkup, on a quiet street near the main theater of Tel Aviv. Dov was a fine roommate, but it's great to be on my own. The new neighborhood is quiet, which I like, but near much busier areas. The maintenance costs are amazingly low compared to New York, all they pay for is a guy to clean the stairway once a week and for maintenance on the solar water heater on the roof.

***

I'm on my way to the airport to pick up my parents. Each summer, IDI hosts a small conference at a hotel. Guests come from all over, including my parents and the Keksts. I have mixed feelings about my parents' visit. It will be nice to see them, but it's a bit of an invasion of my turf; they are donors to IDI, which feels a bit odd. When I see them getting off the plane I say "Welcome to the cultural capital of southwestern Asia!" And Dad says "Israel isn't in Asia." I say "Yes it is." and we go back and forth. When we get to my apartment, I check a map and, of course, Israel is in Asia. He says the map was wrong. That's Dad!

In between sessions at the conference, I amuse myself by playing with kids who are staying at the hotel. On the second day, I'm sitting with my parents and the Keksts and the Carmons at lunch on the terrace of the hotel and I have finished eating, we are just sitting around and talking casually. A little boy, maybe three years old, comes up to me and asks "Can you come play?" Gershon turns to me and says "How do you *do* that?" I don't really know how I do it. It's easy. I had played with that kid the day before at lunch. If you play with kids, they will like you. Easy. But I don't tell Gershon that. He has trouble relating to his own kids, much less strange ones you meet at conferences. However, I think to myself: "OK, Gershon can run a successful PR firm, and make a lot of money, but here is something I can do that he can't; something he doesn't even know how to start to do." And he is not alone. I slowly realize that most adults don't like or understand children.

Kids are easy. They tell you what they want, and what they don't want. It's obvious when they are upset. Adults mask all this stuff because it would be rude to start screaming, or act in such blatant ways. Instead, they use facial expressions and body language (which I can't read), or "nice" rejections. And it's not just bad stuff that I miss. Adults don't come up to you anmd say "can you come play?" and when they flirt, they do it in weird ways instead of just saying what they think.

Of course I go play with the kid. But the conference is really good for me, too. I'm an adult. I'm participating in the conference, not so much as anyone's child, but as an employee and a colleague. I've been talking to adults in a relatively adult way for years, but now I am talking as an adult.

***

On one trip back to New York, in 1986, I see the movie *Stand by Me* about four 12 year old friends who have a traumatic adventure. The movie is told in flashback. It ends out of the flashback with the now grown character of one of the boys saying "I never had any friends later on like the ones I had when I was 12. Jesus. Does anyone?" And that strikes me as very sad about my life, because I never had those 12 year old friends, and I can never have them.

***

I have made friends with a neighbor in the Maon. He is a single father. His son, Seth, is five years old and is almost totally blind. Seth is one of the sweetest kids I ever meet. Of course I offer to babysit.

Seth's dad is out for the night and I'm babysitting. When I tell him it's time for bed, he asks "Is it the time abba said to go to bed?" and I tell him it is. So we get him all ready. Teeth brushed, pajamas on, tucked in and so on. I say "good night, Seth." and he says "good night, Peter." I go in the other room. I hear him call "Peter!" I've babysat before. I know the drill. He wants water. Or it's too warm. Or he needs another story. Or it's too cold. What kid wants to go to bed? I go to his room. "What is it, Seth?" "I want kisses." "OK, Seth. How many kisses do you want?" "I want ten kisses and a matana" (matana is Hebrew for present, we speak a mix of Hebrew and English; Seth's father is American). And I give him 11 kisses. Back out to the other room. "Peter!" "What is it Seth?" "Anni ohev otcha" (I love you.)

***

Like most Israelis, the Limons are totally secular. But, like many Israelis, they often have a Friday night dinner that is more elaborate than their usual dinners. They always have guests, often including me. One Friday night, they also invite Ronit (rhymes with go seat), who is about my age and who they think I will like. I do. She is a sabra (native Israeli) but her parents are from Iraq. She has olive skin and curly dark hair and looks nice. She's also nice. And she seems to like me. She's amazed by the food because, while her family also has Friday night dinners, the food is totally different.

Ronit and me

We start dating a lot right away. We like each other. Her English is about as good as my Hebrew, so we make a deal: She will speak to me in English and I will correct her and I will speak to her in Hebrew and she will correct me. This lasts a little while, but my Hebrew is getting better and we start talking solely in that language. This feels really good. Now I am not only an adult at work, but in a relationship. And we tease each other and flirt with each other and tell each other how wonderful the other one is and so on. This feels good; this feels normal; this feels like what people in a relationship do. My Hebrew gets to the point where I can read *Ha'aretz* (the "good" newspaper, the equivalent of the *New York Times*) with reasonable comprehension. But the only writing I have to do is some checks and filling out the occasional form. I do get a program on my computer that lets me type in Hebrew, but I never get beyond the hunt-and-peck method of using it.

My Hebrew gets good enough that I can tell jokes that are funny (albeit with a strong American accent that I never lose); then it gets good enough that I can hear jokes and tell that they are funny. That feels good too.

I meet her family and they are also nice. I introduce Ronit to Ashkenazi food (gefilte fish, latkes, matzoh ball soup ...) and she introduces me to Iraqi and Mizrachi Jewish food (cigarim, which are cylindrical pastries filled with meat; mlawach which is a Yemenite dish of fried dough, kebabs, and more).

We get pretty close. After we've been dating for a year or so, I invite her to fly back to New York with me and meet my family. She accepts! I don't tell her much about my family. Sure, I tell her that Dad is a successful lawyer and Mom does philanthropic work and that my brother is in the music business. I tell her about their house. But I don't go into details about their personalities or our relationships. I'm not really ready to do it, and my Hebrew isn't quite good enough to capture all the nuance.

They seem to like her OK, but I'm not sure if they would have been cool with me marrying her; at least, my mom might not have been. But, when I start talking to Ronit about marriage, she says she isn't close to being ready to marry and doesn't know when she will be. I want to be married and I want to be a dad. So, after about a year and a half of dating, I break up with her, on very good terms. But, even on good terms, this is hard.

Ronit was quite modest about romantic things. This greatly disappointed me at the time, but, looking back, I have more mixed feelings. A more experienced, willing partner might have overwhelmed me or rejected me or teased me. But she also might have been a good introduction to sex. Instead I was still a virgin when we broke up. Weird. Yes, her culture is different. But it's not like she was from Iraq, herself. She was born and grew up in Israel; she dressed casually, she wasn't religious, so, whatever it was, it wasn't completely cultural. It was something else and I don't know what.

***

I've lived in Israel for three years, and I decide to move back to New York. There's no one big reason. But I've figured out that I will never speak Hebrew the way I speak English. I'm used to being a "beyond fluent" speaker of the language and I will never get to that level in Hebrew. All my friends and colleagues *are* at that level; they are all highly educated, highly literate people.

I'm used to knowing more than the typical person about the history and culture and politics of my country; I will never get to that level in Israel. I'll never really be an educated Israeli. For instance, although nearly all Israelis are secular, they learn about the Bible (well, the old testament, anyway) in school. Literate Hebrew is sprinkled with Biblical allusions the way literate English is sprinkled with Shakespeare. Nearly all those biblical allusions are lost on me.

These things matter to me, a lot. They are a big part of who I am. They are what I'm good at.

Also, all my family is in the USA.

All through the process of deciding to move back and packing, and so on, I think about Israel and its effect on me. Overall, I think it was really good for me. I left a 26 year old boy, I returned a 29 year old man. I had shown myself (and my mother) that I could live on my own, have a job, have a relationship, shop for my own food, do my own laundry, keep my apartment at least clean enough for myself, and so on. I could live without her. I don't know how she felt about that, but I felt good and a little bit more whole.

Chapter 14

Adulthood at last

I am 29 and I'm back from Israel. I realize that New York City is home. Israel had a lot of advantages, but this is my place.

When I first move back from Israel, I live in an apartment that my parents have in the city, but that they almost never occupy, but that is only until I can find my own place. I'm not going from living on my own to living with them, even if they aren't there. Then I move to West 57th street in Manhattan, in an L-shaped studio on the 44th floor of a big building.

Mom gives me a housewarming gift. It is a big, heavy box. I unwrap it. It's a set of Calphalon pots. They are nice pots, but by no means extraordinarily expensive. As she presents them to me, she says "I never owned a whole set of pots." She doesn't say "I hope you use these for many years", nor does she say "I researched and these get high marks" or anything like that. No. She says "I never owned a whole set of pots." So I say "then buy yourself a set!" and I think to myself "you crazy old lady." I haven't got my mother completely figured out, but I'm not letting her lay this kind of crap on me anymore. There's something wrong with her, but I'm going to stop letting it make me miserable. Good for me. Not only will I be less miserable, but it's one more sign that I am growing up.

It's good to be home. It's good to fully understand the language. Sometimes when people ask how good my Hebrew got, I say "In Hebrew, if I hear everything, I understand half, but in English, if I hear half, I understand everything." And it's good to catch people's references, whether to literature or history or whatever. And it's nice to be near my brother and a little closer to my sister.

I let people know that I'm interested in finding a girlfriend. When I tell my parents they have almost no reaction. My brother is more enthusiastic. I have a few first dates, where I always think things are going fine, but the women evidently disagree and never accept another date. On each date, we would go to dinner and it would usually seem to be going very well, to me. We would chat and seem to like each other. The woman would laugh at my jokes. All good things. But then no responses to my calls. I never figured out why. I hear about something called "chemistry" but I don't really know what that is. Apparently, it's important. And apparently, again, something is wrong with me.

By this point, Dad is the senior partner in the largest law firm in the USA, and he and Mom are both in their 60s. While I was in Israel my parents bought a house. This is the first time they've owned a house (although they owned the apartment on 79th Street). They've never found a spot they both like, partly because my father's idea of a very modest abode is my mother's idea of a preposterous mansion. She points out that she will be doing all the cleaning; he doesn't point out that, if she wasn't so uptight and hard to work for, she could hire people to do a lot of it. No, instead, he proposes that she could just get big fans and blow all the dirt out the doors and windows.

The place they find is called Beechwood, in Scarborough, a suburb of New York. It's on an estate that had once belonged to Frank Vanderlip, who was one of the CEOs of Citibank. He died in 1920 with a net worth of $ 20 million (probably about $1 billion today). The estate divided the mansion into three large homes and put up other, smaller houses on the rest of the grounds.

Beechwood

My parents bought one part of the mansion. When they bought it, the attic was full of rooms that had housed Vanderlip's servants. They converted a bunch of those rooms into three nice bedrooms, but that left about 10 tiny rooms which my parents left empty or used for storage. The bottom two floors have a huge dining room, living room, kitchen, and three bedrooms (one of which they use as a study).

***

On one of my trips home from Israel, I was living in one of the three spare bedrooms on the top floor. I was looking for something and open a hall closet. There are about 100 light bulbs stacked neatly on a shelf, all the same wattage and size and everything.

ME: Hey mom! Why do you have so many light bulbs?
MOM: I found them on sale for 5 cents off.

That's Mom, all over. Save $5.00. Get light bulbs for life.
Every Saturday morning I see her sitting at the kitchen table with coupons from from various newspapers spread out all over.

She goes through them carefully, picking out the ones for things she wants to buy, and then she visits three or four different supermarkets, buying chicken in this one and celery in that one, to be sure to spend as little as possible.

I wonder what's going on. Okay, fine. Some people need to save every penny. But she doesn't. I figure she is just putting a low value on her own labor, because she's spending an hour or two or more a week to save a few dollars. I very much doubt she did the actual calculations. Even though she's very smart, having graduated college at 18 after skipping three times in school, math is not her thing. But maybe subconsciously this is what's happening. And what must that be like? Her husband is earning thousands of dollars an hour and she's valuing her time, even subconsciously, at perhaps $ 3 per hour. I don't think she saw it that way, but I really don't know what she was doing.

I don't think a lot of people figure out the time value of their labor this way, but I wonder why they don't; people say it's cheaper to eat home than go out, and, mostly, it is. But that's only if you don't value the time spent shopping, cooking, and cleaning up.

Mom tells me she shops in the bargain basement of Syms, an off-price department store. One time, Larry and Billie Tisch (these are the Tisches of Tisch School of the Arts at NYU, and Tisch Hospital, and so on; Larry is one of my dad's clients and Billie is his wife) are over to a dinner party at Beechwood and Billie admires Mom's dress, whereupon she explains how she had gotten it for an absurdly low price by spending a few hours going through all the clothes in the bargain basement. Billie looked kind of nonplussed at this.

By this point, my mother's narcissistic unnecessary martyr routine is old news to me. But I wonder if she realized how weird she must appear to Billie. I think she must; Mom knows the social rules. It's one thing to save money on clothes (and spend hours doing so), it's another to brag about it to someone who probably spent thousands of dollars on her own clothes. Maybe she just can't help herself.

By now, many of Dad's clients are willing to pay for both of them to travel, first class, to go to meetings. But Mom refuses to fly first class. She flies coach, with my dad in first class on the same plane.

I wonder what drives her to this. Surely some if it is low self-esteem. But maybe some of it is a way of attacking Dad. Dad loves spending money, and she can't stop him. He buys custom made shirts. He eats in expensive restaurants. He's also very charitable, both with his time and money. So, she will buy shirts that are "irregular" for her kids, and shop in bargain basements for herself (however, she has no problems with his charity).

To her friends, Mom was gracious and warm and attentive, but also a model of efficiency. One friend who visited Beechwood took to calling mom "obersturmbahnfuhrer", which was the Nazi rank equivalent to colonel, but he meant it in a vaguely affectionate way. He was teasing her, not insulting her. But she did ask house guests to wake up early on the day they were leaving so that she could wash the sheets when the electric rates were lower.

***

One day I see a book in a bookstore. *Surely You're Joking, Mr. Feynman* by Richard Feynman, the famous physicist and iconoclast. I've been a fan for a while (almost every nerd or geek is a fan of Feynman, especially after his explanation, a couple years earlier, of why the Challenger exploded). I buy the book and take it home and start reading. It's an easy read, much more about his life than about physics. And I see similarities. Of course, there are differences. For one thing, he is much, much smarter than I am. I found out in college that I am good at math, not great at it. He is great at it. And our brains work in almost opposite ways within the math world. He is extremely visual and I am not visual at all. He is also my parents' generation, not mine.

But I see similarities. For instance, he always raises his hand all the time in every class. I raise my hand whenever I can restrain myself from shouting out the answer. He's interested in and curious about all sorts of subjects. Me too. He likes school. Me too. He behaves oddly, sometimes on purpose. Me too.

And he is really, really successful, which is cool. Despite, and maybe even because of, his peculiarities, he is held in high esteem by just about everyone. I know I'm not going to be Feynman. But it's a nice sign that very unusual people can be successful without getting rid of their eccentricities.

***

It's January, 1989. I get a job in the preschool at Rusk Institute for Rehabilitation Medicine. They need help with data and I'm good with data. It's a good job—nice people and a friendly atmosphere and interesting kids, even if I'm not working with them directly. Data analysis is the first job I've had where I'm clearly better than most people, even my very intelligent colleagues. I find this is something I like: I like being around intelligent people who nonetheless need my help.

I do help out a little in the classrooms, mostly if a teacher is on break or out sick or something. One of the little girls is named Miracle. She has no arms and about a half of one leg. And she gets around by sort of using that leg as a kind of pogo stick. The physical therapists say that they had never seen anyone locomote that way and hadn't thought it was possible. A little boy name Luis is a champion of the wheelchair, zipping along the hallways at preposterous speeds, stopping on a dime, and spinning and turning with abandon.

One of my colleagues, Cate, is studying to take the licensing exam in psychology. She's a smart woman (she is done with her PhD in Psych, after all), but she is having a lot of trouble with the test. I ask her to let me see it and I show here how to answer many of the questions, even though I've never had a psychology course.

This is true on many tests, especially multiple choice tests. Often, the answer is obvious or, at least, somewhat clear even if you don't know the material. You just have to realize that the point of the test is getting the right answer, not knowing the right answer.

I wouldn't have done well on the whole test; many of the questions were pure knowledge questions about which psychologist said what, or could have said what, or things like that. But many questions could really only have one answer. She passes the exam and becomes a therapist.

Another colleague, Richard, becomes my friend. We often have lunch together. Sometimes he asks me for advice and I give it; he seems to like or agree with what I say. Mostly we just talk about all sorts of things. Rich is a clinical psychologist and, at one point, he tells me I would make a good clinical psychologist. I say "Rich, I would make a good clinical psychologist for *you* because I like you. But I don't like most people. And I don't understand them."

Richard and I stay friends a while. Leslie and I go to his wedding. But Richard has now disappeared. He moved to Connecticut, but still had an office in New York City. Once, I dropped off a note for him in his building, but I never heard back.

***

***

For the first time ever my father sets me up. I think this is great; he is showing a lot more obvious interest in me as an adult than he ever showed in me as a kid. The woman he sets me up with is named Ellen. She used to be his paralegal but is now in law school. He does it well: He books us a table in one of his favorite restaurants and has the bill paid in advance. It's a fancy Italian restaurant near his office on the East Side of Manhattan.

Ellen and I arrive separately. She is around my age and very attractive, with light brown hair and brown eyes. We get some wine and look at the menus and start talking. The food is really good and the service is attentive without being obsequious (Dad was a big tipper). And he chooses well too. Ellen and I talk and talk. I do sometimes interrupt her, like I do with everyone, but she interrupts me back! This is great! Eventually, we notice that no other patrons are still eating and the waiters are putting the chairs on top of the tables.

I think this is my best first date ever. But, I am wrong all the time. How did she think it went? I don't know. But I ask her out again and she says "Yes." That's a new thing! No one's done that since Ronit. Ellen is close to perfect for me: She's very smart, she loves to talk, she's different enough from me to be interesting but not so different as to be overwhelming, and she's pretty, too.

On our second or third date, Ellen lets me know she is bi. That's OK with me; I'm just happy she's dating me!

On our third or fourth date, after dinner we go back to my apartment and start fooling around, still chatting a lot, gradually getting more and more involved and less and less dressed. I had done only a tiny bit of this with Ronit; I had never seen Ronit naked. So, this is a first! And it is a lot of fun and very exciting in at least two senses of the word. We are both lying naked in bed and telling each other things to do that we like. Then we do them.

However, we don't have sex because I don't have a condom. So, I remain a virgin, but this is the first time that anyone but me touches me sexually or vice versa.

For some reason, it never happens again.

And then, a few months after our first date, she decides she really prefers women to men. This is pretty devastating.

We stay friends for a while. There's a restaurant near my apartment that has a large window facing the street, and we eat and watch women and compare our preferences. Sometime we go to the gym together.

In romance, lots of women say they like funny men. I know I am funny. And they say they like smart men. I'm pretty smart. But they don't like *me*, somehow.

So, that's two romantic relationships by age 30.

> Many years later I realize that a lot of my best relationships are asymmetric. I get along fine with my sister, but she is more like another mother. I get along with my nephews; I am nothing like a father to them, but we get along great. But, again, asymmetric. Even in high school I got along with some teachers and, in college, I got along with almost all my professors—asymmetric again. And I've always done well with therapists, which is about as asymmetric a relationships as two adults can have.

***

I am 30 years old and I decide to seek therapy again because I have almost no relationships, either friendly or romantic. I stopped seeing Dr. Weintrob about 10 years ago. This time, I'm an adult. I ask my friend Phyllis and she recommends Dr. Robert Naiman.

I like him immediately. He is about my parents' age (mid 60s), balding with a fringe of gray hair. He is casually dressed, which I like, and sees me in an office inside his home on Central Park West. Therapy is very different now than it was with Dr. Weintrob because I am very different now than I was then. Not only am I an adult and not a kid, but I am much less troubled and have a much more specific complaint. So, Dr. Naiman is much more critical than Dr. Weintrob was; I couldn't have dealt with criticism from Dr. W.

After I have been seeing him for a while he recommends group therapy, because he wants to see how I interact in a group of people, rather than in the very artificial and constrained relationship of individual therapy.

The group meets first in his office and then the whole group goes (without Dr. Naiman) to one of our apartments where we eat dinner and continue talking. It's a very different experience from individual therapy; we all opine on each other's issues, so everyone gets input from a bunch of people. One nice thing about group is that I learn that there are so many ways to be a functional neurotic. People are in all sorts of relationships that malfunction in all sorts of ways. People figure out ways to hate themselves that I had never dreamed of.

Most people in group have some sort of diagnosis. Mine is learning disabled. But when I tell people that, they say things like "How can you be learning disabled when you are good at reading and good at math?" or "How can you be learning disabled and have a Ph.D.?" or even a flat-out "You are not learning disabled". This is stupid. It's as if they think the only things you learn on the journey to adulthood are reading and math! But a newborn is capable of very little. They can pee and they can suck. They can't even focus their eyes or smile. Everything else that adults do is learned. And you can be LD in any of it. I try to explain my LD to them, but it's hard to explain; I don't fully understand it, myself, and still haven't found any specific label or diagnosis that would apply to me. But I do know that there are many things that I am very bad at.

On my third or fourth week, we decide it's time for them to come to my apartment for the first time they ask why I don't have anything on the walls. I said "what should be there?" It's not like I had thought about hanging some paintings or whatever and then rejected the idea, I just hadn't though of it at all, so, all the walls are white and blank. I also didn't think of getting the walls painted. White was fine. People tell me that art belongs there. People have art on the walls. That's just what people do. My lack of art is, in fact, one aspect of my LD.

***

Somewhere in here, I stop being angry at my mother and start pitying her. I start looking at her as a fellow adult. I realize that she is a woman who has what pretty much anyone on Earth would consider a good life. No. A great life. And she is miserable and angry a lot of the time. How sad!

The reduction in anger is gradual; it peaked in adolescence and has been diminishing ever since. But the notion of feeling sorry for her is relatively sudden and is almost an epiphany. And once it happens, it's seismic. This is another big step in becoming an adult and in becoming less miserable myself. And it's a step toward becoming able to forgive her.

> *Eventually, I will figure out that forgiveness is about the person doing the forgiving, not the person who is being forgiven. Forgiving is a way of moving on with your life and denying the other person power over you. And it's a way to heal, which is part of being whole.*

Chapter 15

My 30s—Romance, more school, work

I am 30 years old and one February day I get a phone from my Aunt Flo, who is following in her brother's footsteps and getting involved in my dating life for the first time. "There's a woman who is waiting to hear from you. Her name is Leslie and her number is XXX-XXXX". I'm pretty excited "waiting to hear from me" sounds promising.

So, the next day, I call. "Hi, this is Peter." There's no response. Did I dial wrong? Is my aunt crazy? Does Leslie not want to talk to me? I continue "My aunt, Florence Hersch, suggested I call."

"I don't know anyone named Florence Hersch." Now it's my turn to be silent. What's going on? There's a long pause and then "Wait a minute. A few months ago, my mother said someone might call."

I'm thinking *a few months ago? Someone might call?* but I continue: "Well, let's pretend I'm him and go to dinner."

She agrees. Cool! But I've had first dates before, so I try to restrain my enthusiasm. I don't tell anyone I have a date, except my therapist. We set a date and she picks an Indian restaurant near her apartment. Indian isn't my favorite, but I'm glad she at least picked something from another continent, we are in New York, why eat American?

The night of our first date, I put on a sport coat and slacks and go to pick her up at her apartment on West 82nd street, where she lives with her mother. I'm nervous. None of my other first dates have involved going to someone's apartment, we've always met at a restaurant. That must be a good sign, right? But I get the address wrong. I call her from a pay phone to find out where she lives. Oh. 82nd street. I'm on 83rd. Good thing I'm habitually early. I ring the bell and she opens the door. The first thing I notice is that she's very short. She describes herself as "5 foot minus." But she looks nice; she has wavy dark brown hair. She smiles and I smile and we say hello and head off to the restaurant.

The streets are icy. Neither of us is the most coordinated person in the world. Leslie's father Eddie will later describe us walking together as "two moons orbiting each other." Getting to the restaurant is a bit of an adventure, even though it's not far. But we make it. As we're eating, I'm thinking, this seems to be going well, but I always think dinner is going well and it never is. But then Leslie says "How about dessert at Cafe Lalo?" That's got to be a good sign! She wants to keep talking to me! And she likes dessert! Well, who doesn't like dessert? Still, it's a good thing.

We keep talking easily while eating cake. After that, I suggest that we go back to my place, even though her place is a lot closer, because I live alone. She says "yes" again! Another good sign.

We start dating pretty regularly. Leslie doesn't actually move in with me, but a lot of her stuff is at my apartment, and so is she. After all this time, I'm glad this is happening! Ronit and I never made love and she didn't ever sleep over. 30 is really late for this to happen, but it is good. We have fun together. We like a bunch of the same things. I like her friends and they seem to like me. And, for me, it's enough. I like Leslie. We are comfortable with each other.

All this is good. But I find myself wondering why it isn't even better. I've read about people in love, with their extravagant, over-the-top feelings, and what I'm experiencing with Leslie isn't that. But it's enough. We agree on big things: We both want kids and we both really like kids. Like me, Leslie was a baby sitter and a camp counsellor (unlike me, she liked her own camping experience). We have similar notions of how to raise children. Neither one of us is a neat freak. Both of us are prompt. We both dress casually as a usual thing.

Two big aspects of adulthood are having a job and being in a relationship. I've got both! Cool!

***

Jason and I are, more or less by chance, living in the same apartment building. He moved in after I did, so maybe it was deliberate on his part, I don't know. One day, after Leslie and I have been dating a few weeks, I figure it's time for her to meet him. He will be much easier than my parents! I've told Leslie a bit about him and about us and I've told Jason about Leslie.

Leslie agrees to meet him. I take her down to his apartment. It's OK for a first meeting, I guess, but they don't really hit it off. In the elevator ride back up, she says "You two are from different planets, aren't you?" I nod and agree. We are. We always have been.

The next day, when I ask Jason what he thinks, he says "well, she makes you happy."

One thing that worries me a little but is also nice is that Leslie and I have very different skills. I'm good at math and science and research and schoolwork in general. She is good at art and interpersonal relationships. I figure this will all come in handy if we get married and have kids! They will know who to ask about what.

***

CHAPTER 15. MY 30S—ROMANCE, MORE SCHOOL, WORK

It's Passover. Our first holiday together. We are invited to my cousin Denny's house. Jason and his girlfriend will be there; so will Stuart (Denny's brother) and his wife Laurie; and various younger cousins. But my parents will be there, and they are going to be the problem. Before we accept the invitation I warn Leslie about them. I tell her "Dad won't talk to you, but don't take it personally, because he is like that with everyone." I've already told her enough about my dad that she can sort of see that. Then I say "Mom can be difficult. She might not talk to you either. Mom knows she is supposed to." We had talked a lot about our mutual parents, in any case. I've met her mom and dad with no particular issues arising. Leslie didn't have to issue warnings ahead of time.

Sandy, her mom, is a nice, middle aged woman. Her dad, Eddie, is funny. Leslie gets embarrassed by him, and I can see that, but, to me, he's amusing. For instance, she tells me that once, on an escalator in Penn Station, he turned to a stranger and said "Are we in New York???"

As we get ready to go to Denny's house, I am not too nervous. I'm glad I warned Leslie about my parents. She also seems relatively relaxed, but I don't know for sure. When we get to Denny's house, Lori invites Leslie into the kitchen to help with the cooking and, tells her she wants to "remove her from the scrimmage". Not a bad metaphor for dinner in this group, and moreso when you add Dennis to the mix as he is the lone conservative.

We all sit down around the big dining table. One of Mom's traits is forming opinions of people in the first few minutes of meeting them and not changing those opinions later. As we eat, it becomes clear that Leslie does not meet with Mom's approval, since Mom isn't talking to her. This doesn't bother me. Leslie is my girlfriend, not hers! But I wonder how much it bothers Leslie. I don't react during dinner; what would I do? "Hey! Mom! I like Leslie. We're dating a lot. Could you *talk* to her?" I don't think so. Maybe normal people would figure out something to say, but I don't. (My mother does talk to Jason's girlfriend Wendy;

it's pretty clear already that she likes Wendy more than she likes Leslie.)

Despite all this, we stay a while and it seems to be more or less OK. Other people there do talk to Leslie.

Later, when we are back at my apartment and sitting and talking about it, Leslie tells me that, as I had said, she didn't get a negative feeling from my dad, but that my mom was being deliberately rude; I mean, it's very impolite to not talk to someone all evening! Neither one spoke to her hardly at all, but, somehow, my dad gave a very different vibe than my mom. My mother knows the rules of civil behavior and has broken them on purpose; my father either doesn't know the rules or doesn't care about them at all. He never has. And he gets away with it partly because he's honest about it but partly because he's who he is; he's a genius and he makes millions and millions of dollars for his clients.

Leslie doesn't say this, but I think she's concerned about Mom not liking her; I mean, no one likes being judged negatively, but Leslie seems more affected by it than some people. She worries a lot about people liking and not liking her. But she does thank me for warning her.

***

Leslie and I often play games and eat and drink with a group of her friends. About six of us are doing this at my place. Leslie and I are on the couch, other people are on chairs and whatever. We are playing *Scattergories* in which you get a topic and a letter of the alphabet and each person has to write down things that fit the topic and start with the letter. Then you get points for making choices that no one else does. The category is "women's names" and the letter is "L" and we both choose "Lorelei." Everybody goggles at us and starts making comments about how much of a coincidence this is and how that must mean we are on the same wavelength. I mean, first, right here is *Leslie* which is, after all a woman's name that starts with L. But there's Lainie or Linda or Lucy or Lila (Leslie has an aunt Lila ...) *Lorelei?*

Even though we've only been dating a few months, I start thinking about proposing. I know that's a big step, I know it's only been a few months. And I know what I'm feeling doesn't quite match what I read and hear about. But I want to be married. And I've been looking for a romantic partner for a decade, with very little success. If I don't move on this relationship, maybe it will disappear. Would it take me *another* decade to find another partner? That wouldn't be good at all.

On July 4 weekend (five months after we met) we visit my cousin Stuart in the Hamptons on Long Island. Since neither of us drive, we take the Hampton Jitney back to the city (it was actually the Hampton Express, but "jitney" is such a great word, and there *was* a Hampton Jitney). It's a long trip (there is always a lot of traffic on that route, especially on summer weekends).

I casually ask: "What kind of wedding do you like?" never exactly saying it's *our* wedding I'm talking about. She likes relatively formal, traditional, weddings. So do I. By the end of the trip, I'm pretty sure I've proposed and I'm pretty sure she has said "yes" and that we are engaged.

This feels really good. But I'm not certain. I didn't *actually* ask her. She didn't *actually* say "yes". So, on the same bus trip, I write a poem for her in my head, ending in "say you'll be my wife."

When we get home, I write it down. Then we have dinner and go to sleep.

The next morning, I read it to her in bed. She says "Yes." We're engaged! And we celebrate in bed. I feel good.

I'm sitting at home with Leslie and I call Mom to tell her we are getting married. After congratulating me, she says we should have it on their lawn at Beechwood. It is a very nice lawn but I don't commit one way or another, as we haven't made any plans yet, I'm just letting her know that her elder son is tying the knot.

***

It's 1989, and my boss's boss at Rusk tells me that I have a good future in the data analysis field but that I would need a PhD to get promoted. I decide to get a degree in psychology, which has always interested me, and specialize in psychometrics. This is the study of latent traits. A latent trait is one that can't be measured directly. For instance, if you want to measure a person's height, you can do so by standing them against a wall, putting a mark at the top of their head, then using a tape measure to see how far that is off the ground. But you can't do that with a person's intelligence, or personality, or readiness for a job. Those traits are latent and measuring them is complex. I find it fascinating, partly for the statistics and math behind it, but also because of the weird patterns of my own test scores and because of their importance in my life. For a few years, I have had vague thoughts of creating better instruments for measuring different kinds of learning disability; studying psychometrics is the route to doing that.

But first, I decide to get an MA at NYU, since it is familiar and accessible and I want to be sure of what I'm doing before I start the Ph.D. I wind up liking psychometrics.

***

I'm getting married! 20 or 25 years ago, if you had bet that Peter would be married, you could have gotten big odds. I might have bet against it, myself. As the time passes and the plans get more solid, I keep on reminding myself that I'm getting married. That feels good. That feels grown-up.

It's later that summer. I am 30 years old and Leslie and I are planning our wedding. We decide on a date: June 16th. June weddings! Maybe we will get lucky and have gorgeous weather. We are having a traditional wedding in the traditional month. That feels good. One decision made.

CHAPTER 15. MY 30S—ROMANCE, MORE SCHOOL, WORK

We talk about my Mom's offer, but we want to have it at a more traditional venue. We visit various sites. All the places we look at are excellent and it feels good to be making these plans; I mean, the actual process is a bit tiresome. The different places *all* seem nice. They all seem similar. After a few visits, they all seem to mush together in my head.

We finally decide on the Water Club on the East River; it's gorgeous and it literally floats on the river, with amazing views of both the water and New York. It can hold plenty of people. It's famous for hosting weddings. It will be a great site. And they have space on June 16th. So, that's done too! We've got a site!

Now, there's only the guest list.

We make these decisions pretty easily, even though (from what I've heard) a lot of couples have fights about the site and the date. We don't. We discuss things and voice our opinions and come to agreement pretty easily. That's a big relief!

I'm sitting with Leslie and I call my mother again to tell her that we've picked a site and date. I don't say "We are thinking of having it at the Water Club". Nor do I say "We would like to have it at the Water Club". I say "We have decided to have it at the Water Club."

She says "I regard it as an open question." That is Mom, all over. We argue. She points out how nice the lawn is. I point out that it could rain. She says we could move it into the ballroom. I say we want more people than it can hold. She says they could put up tents. We get off the phone with it still unresolved. Leslie was listening to all this, but only heard my side.

Leslie and I talk. We really want the Water Club. Mom and I argue. She won't give in. Leslie and I realize that she will fight us about everything. She wants to be in control. Leslie and I talk some more and agree that she would do a good job. She's better at that sort of thing than either of us; she's better at this kind of thing than the vast majority of people. Neither of us wants to fight with her over every detail.

We agree to get married on her lawn. We agree to just let her run most of it, although we do pick our own musicians. She accepts victory rather grudgingly.

Mom gives us a maximum number that will fit and Leslie and I make a guest list. And the planning is easy. We don't fight about the guest list or anything else, really. There's no one she wants to invite that I don't, or vice versa. The only fights are with my mom, about who *she* wants to invite. It's my wedding, not hers! I like lots of her friends, but not all of them. I've been disagreeing with my mom for years. Some of the time my disagreement was silent, sometimes it was loud. But now it's mature. I do manage to get my way on most of the decisions, but there is one guy who is very close to them who I really don't like at all and haven't since I was a kid. She insists he has to be invited.

We send Mom the final list.

She calls me up and asks "Who are all these Sobels and Beyers?" and I say "They are Leslie's family!" Sheesh!

I hang up and look at the guest list. We hadn't counted up who had invited more people, although we knew it was roughly equal. But when my mother made that ridiculous comment, I decided to count. Guess what? There are more Flom tables than Beyer tables. I don't tell Mom this, it's not really her business. It's not her wedding.

***

Before the wedding people tell me things. A lot of people tell me I won't be able to eat at the wedding. People tell me I will be very stressed out. People tell me I have to dance. But I've never danced. I have no sense of rhythm, ever since Rudolf Steiner. I still can't clap in time with music, much less move the rest of my body in time to the music. Leslie and I do argue about this, but not too much. Leslie makes a lot of good points: It's traditional, I don't have to look good dancing, it's a wedding, and so on. My only point is that I really don't want to dance and I will look ridiculous. I do wind up dancing the hora for a little bit.

***

It's June 16. The big day. It's forecast to be one of the hottest June days in New York City history and many of our parents' friends and relatives are not that young.

Leslie and I came up to my parents' house last night. I'm sitting in the kitchen with Mom and the phone rings. It's the florist. I hear Mom say "Well, *I* am the groom's mother and if you will shut up and listen to me, I will tell you how to get here!" We're lucky he didn't dump the flowers in a lake. (My parents' house isn't easy to find, and many people get lost trying to find it).

Part of my parents' lawn is on a hill, and, at the bottom of the hill, there is a stone walkway under a colonnade. I'm standing at the center with about 100 guests in front of me (including Nancy and Jason and Sabha). Leslie is wearing a beautiful white gown and looks wonderful. I am wearing a navy blue suit. Her dad walks her down the pergola to me, where I'm standing under a chuppah. Despite what people said, I'm not stressed out much at all. I'm kind of excited.

Bride and groom

The Wedding Aisle

Michael, the same rabbi who performed my bar mitzvah and who has been a friend all these years, performs the ceremony, which is fairly traditional. Then it's "I do" and Leslie and I kiss. We're married! Then we all move up the lawn to tables where lunch will be served.

But before lunch, it's time for speeches. Buena, Leslie's maid of honor, starts off her speech with "When I first met Leslie, I didn't like her." This reminds me that, after our second or third date, Leslie had told me she didn't like me until dessert at Cafe Lalo. Jason also gives a speech, then my dad does, and then I do. Despite what people told me, I eat fine.

After lunch, it's time for wedding cake. Ours is chocolate cake with chocolate icing, which my mother made herself, for 100 or so people. It's got seven tiers, from a very large base tapering to a small top tier. It's decorated with candy flowers and raspberries. But, under that, it's the same cake from *The Joy of Cooking* that Mom and I used to bake all the time, just a lot more of it! There's quite a bit of architecture, since all the layers have to stay up. Mom had to store the layers in the freezer and then defrost and ice them and then stack them.

Bride and groom and cake and champagne

***

Most of the guests have departed and we move to my parents' porch, which is sheltered. That's a good thing, because, as so often happens on summer days, a deluge begins in the late afternoon. More guests depart and it's down to just families and the members of the wedding party. We move into the solarium in my parents's house. It's a fairly large room, and we are sitting in a big, vague circle.

As we're all talking, I realize that Mom is drunk. I've never seen that before. She's telling Buena, who she had only met a few times, that she loves her. I'm thinking that her three kids are sitting there and she's never said anything like that to any of us. I'm not entirely sober, myself, but I am angry at her and very glad to be married and moving on from Mom in more ways. Being with Leslie makes it easier to ignore Mom and I'm thinking that being married will make it even easier.

***

It's September, 1992, Leslie and I have been married for just over a year. It's going well, I like being married. I'm going to Fordham University in the Bronx to get my PhD in psychometrics. The campus is small, only 85 acres, and all my classes are in one building, but it's my first time on a traditional campus, with buildings interconnected by curved paths and quads and so on. I keep getting lost going to or from the deli. This is weird. And very frustrating. How can I be getting lost *again*? It's not that big a campus. Normal people find their way. Or they get a little lost and then look at a campus map and figure it out. They certainly don't get lost multiple times going from one place to another.

My disabilities enrage me. And it's worse because I don't know what they are. I've tossed "minimal brain dysfunction" out the window ages ago, when I realized I was smarter than many of my teachers. I learned the new label "learning disabled." But I don't even fit *that* precisely. I didn't exactly fit at Gateway. My scores on the WISC were really weird. I hear about some specific learning disabilities, but I don't have dyslexia — I read very well. I don't have dyscalculia — math is a strength.

But what *do* I have?

One reason I'm interested in psychometrics is that I have vague ideas of coming up with a test that will identify me and others like me. But I find the statistics part of psychometrics more interesting that the test construction. Also, in order to make a test to diagnose people like me, I'd have to figure out what it is that's wrong. And I still don't know what that is.

I somehow make some friends; one of my classmates, John, is a big extrovert and puts together a group of people. One Saturday night in my first year a bunch of us and our plus ones go out for dinner and drinks at an Italian restaurant. I have to get up early the next day, so I leave early, but Leslie stays because she is having a good time and doesn't need to get up early. The next day, some of my friends express surprise that I "let" Leslie stay. They wonder if I trust her. I'm flummoxed by this. Why would I marry someone I didn't trust? Do people do that? And what's with "let"? She's a grown up! She can do what she wants.

***

It's 1992. The Palm Pilot has just been invented. I get one and I love it. This was really pretty life changing for me. People who had tried to get me to be more organized had recommended various paper-based solutions. This usually involved a date book, and an address book, and a phone book, and more. You had to carry them all! And write things down. And then, you had to go and look for what you were supposed to do. And, of course, I lost the books, or forgot them, or didn't write things down, or forgot to refer to things and ... if I did manage to do all that, I couldn't read what I wrote! Now, all that in one place, all entered digitally. No more showing up places on the wrong day, or the wrong time. I still show up way early, but at least I know I'm early and can sit with a book.

Also, there's a new trend for coffee bars. They're everywhere! So now I have a lot more places to sit and read when I'm early.

Even though I don't know what's wrong with me, I am finding some ways around my particular deficits.

***

One of my friends, Michele, is studying to be a clinical psychologist and needs practice giving the WAIS (the adult version of the

CHAPTER 15. MY 30S—ROMANCE, MORE SCHOOL, WORK

test I took as a 5 year old). She wants people who are unusual, so I eagerly volunteer.

Like the WISC, the WAIS has a bunch of subtests, covering different types of intelligence. Block design has you try to imitate a pattern using blocks. In visual puzzles, you are shown a card with three images and one blank space and are asked to pick an image for the blank space.

I take the test in Michele's office. Unlike the WISC back when I was a kid, this time the test and results aren't really important. I know a lot about the test, since I'm studying psychometrics. I'm having fun and also joking around with Michele. I know in advance what is coming and I know which subtests I will have problems with and which ones I will do well on. I'm doing Michele a favor, but I'm also curious to see what exactly my scores will be. I've always liked taking this sort of test, but now, I'm totally relaxed. Although it's fun, I'm serious when answering the questions.

As on the WISC, I do very badly (the equivalent of about an IQ of 70) on some subtests and very well on others. On "information" I get the equivalen of about 160 and on arithmetic, my result is unscorable because I answer some questions before Michele is done asking the question. I simply figure out the question, and then the answer. Doesn't everyone do that?

The arithmetic section is timed and that's not in the manual.

Hey! She *asked* for someone who was unusual! She does show me my scores—they range from 70 to "unscorable"; a little higher than the WISC, but the same weird pattern.

I still don't know what's wrong with me or what my diagnosis should be. But I do learn part of it. When you look at the results on the subtests of an IQ test such as the WAIS, there are three things you can examine: Level, scatter, and pattern.

Level is the average: How high are your scores? Scatter is the amount of variation from highest to lowest. And pattern is which ones are high and low. My average is a bit above average, but not extraordinary. My scatter is extremely broad and my pattern is just weird.

Even in the PhD program, I find most of the class work fairly easy, even routine. I see some of my classmates studying all the time and I wonder what they are studying. OK, some of them are the sort of person who can't help studying all the time. "Oh my God! I might not get the best grade in every class!" I'm not like that, and I don't get the best grade in every class. But I need a 3.5 GPA to keep my fellowship and I'm never in danger of not getting it.

***

One day in class a woman sitting next to me starts to say "did you get dressed in the dark?" but changes mid-question to ask "you didn't want to wake Leslie up, right?"

I look down and see that my tee shirt is on inside out. I didn't get dressed in the dark. I just didn't notice the shirt was wrong.

***

At Fordham, there are three stages to a dissertation. First, there is the proposal. Then the progress report. Then the dissertation defense itself. For my dissertation, I decide to do an analysis of the data from "Terman's Termites", a group of gifted children who Lewis Terman had identified in the 1920s and followed for decades. I'm fascinated; I have always been interested in academically precocious kids. I read a lot of the extensive literature about these kids, and I'm getting excited about applying some advanced and relatively new statistical methods to the extensive data. I turn in my proposal. It's going to be great! It might even get published in a good journal.

After the committee has had time to review the proposal, there is a meeting. My proposal gets turned down. The committee has a few issues that I could have dealt with, but one was that Terman's study was racist. It was. But, as I think to myself and express to

CHAPTER 15. MY 30S—ROMANCE, MORE SCHOOL, WORK

my friends, it was also a 60 year longitudinal study! I wonder what people in 2055 would think of the studies being done at the end of the 20th century. I don't know what they would find wrong, but I guarantee it will be a lot.

I tell some friends about the rejection and that I intend to get drunk, and they have to get me home. They agree. We go to The White Horse in Greenwich Village, one of our usual spots. This is a pretty famous spot; it was Dylan Thomas's favorite bar in New York and it has its own Wikipedia page. But it's mostly a fairly typical bar, offering a variety of drinks and some food. Wooden tables, a tin ceiling, a long bar with stools.

We go there and I get really drunk, I don't usually drink heavily and I don't usually like being drunk, but tonight, I keep drinking, mostly vodka and beer. My friends drink their usual amounts and they do indeed, help me get home, and get the key in the door. I go to sleep and sleep a long time. I wake up around noon and I'm not hung over. (I don't get hangovers, I just sleep through them. Good thing I don't particularly like being drunk). Then I start figuring out a second dissertation.

***

I've been working at Fordham while I'm taking classes, first as a teaching assistant and then as an adjunct professor, but in June of 1995 I see an ad for a job at Consumer's Union (these are the people who publish *Consumer's Reports*. It looks pretty good. It's a new position, doing various kinds of data analysis. I apply and I get it. It's in Yonkers, NY and the commute is a bit of a pain in the neck because I don't drive. First I take a subway, then Metro North, then a van from the company picks us up. Other than that, it's a good job with lots of nice people.

***

Leslie and I have been trying to get pregnant for about a year. We try various things but nothing is happening. So, Leslie goes through a bunch of tests. They don't find any problem. The doctors conclude it isn't her and might be me. Off to the urologist we go.

The first step is getting a sperm count. Looking at pictures of naked women is fun. But the next step is getting a testicular biopsy which is no fun at all.

It was me. No swimmers. The doctor told me with a great bedside manner "well ... You're not having babies!" Looking at the detailed tests, I am completely azospermatic (no sperm at all), which is pretty rare. There's nothing to be done about it.

I've known I wanted to be a dad since before I knew how that happens. I'm pissed at the doctor for telling me so badly and I'm pissed in general because I'm not making any sperm and there's nothing to do about it. Right after this, our relationship changes. We're still committed to each other, but the physical element disappears.

Then we try to adopt, and that is another long process ending in our losing a newborn baby girl when her father shows up on a motorcycle to get her and her mom, after having been absent the entire pregnancy. That messes me up big time, I get suicidal and also furious at the father, but we get through that and it's another sign of why I married Leslie: She deals with this much better than I do, and deals well with me dealing with it badly.

But this is the end of the 20th century, and other methods exist. Leslie is willing to go for IVF and a sperm donor, but I'm not. I have one common and one odd misbelief. I'm not sure the baby will be mine, which seems sensible enough, but I also think that the IVF is like rape, which makes no sense at all. Rape is sex without consent. This isn't sex and it's with consent—indeed, more than consent.

But I overcome these objections.

Then we discuss whether the donor should be someone we know or a stranger. At first I think it should be someone we know, but Leslie thinks that's odd and it is her body that's going to host the baby. She also thinks it will be odd to have the donor in our lives. She convinces me that an anonymous donor is best.

We search for a donor by looking through a catalog and find one we really like. Leslie gives me first pick, since it's my genes that will be missing; so, as I flip through the pages of donor profiles, I try to find one who is academically smart, and funny. Leslie approves of my choice. At the start of December, 1995, a glorified turkey baster gets used. Now we just have to wait.

My dad often takes the whole family on vacation each Christmas. This year, he takes me, my brother, our wives, and my niece to Hawaii. We bring pregnancy tests. Since Leslie is who she is, we bought lots of tests.

And, in a hotel room in Hawaii, in January 1996, we find out that yes, she has been well basted (on the first try!)

***

On one visit to the obstetrician, Leslie gets a sonogram and the technician asks us if we want to know the sex. We both say we do. She says "You're sure you don't want to be surprised?" And I say "There's not much room for surprise." It's a boy! Leslie and I start talking about names. But each of us keeps finding some flaw in whatever name either of us suggest. So, we decide to put off deciding.

It's August, 1996, three weeks before the due date. I'm sitting at my desk at Consumers' Union. I get a call from Leslie that her Dr. Rodke, her ob-gyn, says it is time. The fetus doesn't have a calendar, after all. I call a cab and get to the hospital as fast as I can. It's not an emergency, things are under control, but it's time for him to be born. I'm a little nervous and very excited. A long time ago, Leslie had a brain tumor and there is a shunt going from her brain to her stomach. She's been fine for decades, but the doctors tell us that labor might cause fluid to go back up the shunt into her head. So, she has a planned c-section.

Now, it's time to pick a name. I get to the hospital and see a very pregnant Leslie in her hospital gown sitting in a chair. "How about 'Gabriel' "? I say. And she says 'OK'.

They wheel Leslie into the operating room. I put on a gown and a hood and a mask. Leslie gets put on the operating table and is given an epidural. I'm sitting by her head, holding her hands, and there is a sheet blocking her view of her body from the chest down.

DR. RODKE: Are you squeamish?
ME: No.
DR. RODKE: Then stand up and watch your son being born.

So I stand up and now I'm looking over the sheet and watching what's going on. It's like "Alien". Only native.

I've seen plenty of newborns. Even for a newborn, Gabriel has a scrawny body and a huge head. Then the nurse puts him in my arms and I float higher. It is the first remotely mystical experience of my life. I have this overwhelming feeling that he is MINE. Any doubts that donor insemination would produce a baby who was, somehow, not mine, disappear. I so happy I'm floating. Twenty-six years later he is still mine and I am still aloft.

They tell us that Gabe's head size is in the 98th percentile and his birth weight in the 2nd.

Right after the birth, Leslie gets very sick. She has severe preeclampsia and almost dies. Her blood pressure soars to very dangerous levels and she stays in the ICU for several days and in the hospital for a week. Gabriel is fine, but he stays in the hospital too so he can at least visit his mom. I visit a lot. In the hospital, Gabriel is much calmer than the other babies and cries very little. Looking at him, I see him thinking "what are you all crying about?"

Since Leslie is taking medications that give her hallucinations, we figure breast feeding is out. The nurses are handling the feedings, but on the second day I tell them I want to feed him. They

CHAPTER 15. MY 30S—ROMANCE, MORE SCHOOL, WORK

ask "Do you need help?" but I've held and fed very young babies before, so I know what to do: You put the baby on your forearm, and you make sure you support the head and the tushie. I do that and then I put the bottle in his mouth and he is happily sucking away when, after a minute, a huge spume of formula comes spewing out of him.

I'm pretty freaked out anyway, what with a brand-new newborn and a wife who might die. I'm spending a lot of time in the ICU (not recommended, it's a very noisy, busy place) and some more time in the nursery (much nicer, but also not exactly calm). and this formula fountain is upsetting. I thought I knew what I was doing!

The nurses (who like me because I visit so much) show me what went wrong. With a normal newborn, what I did would have been just right. But Gabe was so small that, by supporting his head on the crook of my elbow, I had closed his throat. He couldn't swallow! They showed me how to put his head so it was over my elbow, with the back of his head against the joint of my elbow. That worked.

After a few days Leslie is moved out of the ICU into a regular room. Then after a few more days, she is recovered (or, at least, is as recovered as most women who just had a c-section) and we head home. And I'm doing much better now; now all I've got is the worries of the father of a newborn, not the worries of a potential solo father of a newborn and a widower.

***

Mom comes for a visit after a little while. We are standing around in the living and talking and she sees pictures of her grandson on our shelves. These were very basic newborn photos, in very plain frames, but still, it's her grandson! Does she say "he is the cutest baby in the history of the world."? No. Does she say "What a great picture?" No. She says "You shouldn't display these. He doesn't look good. He's so skinny." And I say "If we wanted pictures of beautiful people we would clip them out of magazines." I'm well into the phase where I pity my mother, rather than getting angry with her. It was even sort of amusing in a sad way. Who looks at their grandchild and says "don't display the picture"? While I'm not great at reading Leslie's mood, I don't think this bothers her too much either. After all, she says that Gabe "looks like a condor chick." But it feels so different when she says it.

***

Meanwhile, I'm still working at CU. It's still a pretty good job, but it's a long commute and it's a pain in the neck with a baby. I start looking for a new job and find what looks like a good one at NDRI, which is an acronym for National Development and Research Institutes, which tells you nothing. They do research into illicit drug use and the spread of HIV/AIDS and other sexually transmitted diseases. They are in the World Trade Center, which isn't that close to my apartment but is a relatively easy commute on the 1 train.

My first interview at NDRI is with Benny Jose (rhymes with nose), who will be my boss if I get the job. Benny is young guy from India and has an Indian accent. He seems nice but this interview is pretty standard. There are tests to take and forms to fill out and Benny asks the usual sort of questions. As he walks me to my next interview, I think it went pretty well, but nothing special. Benny drops me off at his boss's office. Sam Friedman is middle aged and dressed in a sweat shirt and pants. He's sitting, leaning back in his chair so much that it looks like he will tip over.

I take a seat and he says "I'm going to keep asking you questions until you can't answer them."

I say "Sounds good to me."

He asks a lot of questions and I keep answering them, sometimes with "I don't know." Sometimes he disagrees with my answer and we argue. What a great interview! I like Sam and he seems to like me. He doesn't ever get me to stop answering. Then it's back to Benny who bid me farewell and says he will let me know in about a month. I'm fairly optimistic. I figure that, if it had been really bad, they would have let me know then and there, or, at least, said they would contact me in a few days. If they need a month, then I must be in a pool of candidates who made it through a first interview.

Two or three days later my phone rings and it's Benny "Would you like to have good news from me?" he asks. "Sure" I say, and he tells me they want to hire me right away. I give notice at Consumers and start work at NDRI. Benny is always warning me about Sam "Don't worry" he says "you will get used to Sam." I want to say "I *am* used to Sam! I grew up with Sam! I have to get used to you." In fact, Sam reminds me of my dad in a lot of ways. Both of them are geniuses. Both of them are legends in their fields (Sam's field is networks and spread of disease). Both of them are argumentative. And, importantly for me and my disability, both say exactly what they think. Benny is much more difficult to figure out. He is very polite and correct and reserved. I have no idea when he is pleased or displeased with my work. This is clear, even from the interview: Benny does a good job, but he does a very usual job. His questions could come from a book about how to interview people. Sam writes his own book. Benny is dressed in a button down shirt and nice slacks. Sam is dressed in jeans and a sweatshirt. I never learn Benny's politics; I quickly find out that Sam is a Marxist.

My first project is DUHRAY: Drug Use and HIV Risk Among Youth. The fieldwork is done in Bushwick, Brooklyn, but I rarely go there. I sit in my cubicle and push buttons.

Whenever I give a presentation at a conference about our results (e.g. the American Public Health Association, or the International Society for Sexually Transmitted Disease Research), people will ignore the content and just ask about him. "You work with Sam?" "What is Sam like?" and so on. I tell them "Sam is fine", or "he is good to work with" and stuff like that.

My job is to help with statistical analysis and I keep getting promoted. I start as a senior research associate; in 1999, I become a principal research associate, then, in 2000 they make me director of the statistics support group then (2001) assistant director of the statistics and data analysis core, and then, finally, also in 2001, a senior data manager. Some of these are in parallel with others. I'm told that I could become a research scientist and run entire grants, but I don't want that. I like doing the data analysis and consulting about it.

However, NDRI is a nonprofit and the promotions don't come with big raises. Eventually, I'm a sort of roving data analyst helping out on all sorts of projects while my main duty is to work for Sam. It's a very collegial group. We all know that Sam is in charge, but he treats us much more like colleagues than subordinates and is able to recognize that each of us knows about some things that he doesn't.

As I said, NDRI is in the World Trade Center. There are many exits and entrances to the building and it is located way downtown, where New York City is not a grid and the streets are not numbered. Even though I work there for years, I still get lost all the time.

While at NDRI I study social network analysis. Very briefly, a network is a collection of nodes, some or all of which are connected by lines. One nice property of these networks is that the nodes and lines can be just about anything. For instance, the nodes could be "15th and 16th century Italian noble families" and the lines could represent "marriage". Or the nodes could be "major 20th century corporations" and the lines could show companies sharing a corporate board member. At NDRI, the nodes are people and the lines are "having sex or sharing needles for drug injection" which are two of the most common ways of spreading HIV.

There are a lot of different measures associated with networks. Some measure how connected a network is. Some measure how far it is from one member to another; in fact, Sam says we should call one of our studies "how many steps to the governor's daughter?" to emphasize that these sex and drug networks reach everywhere. But I realize one measure that is missing is one to show the amount of connection between two sub-networks, one of which is infected and the other is not.

I decide to invent such a measure. I start working on it right away. This is just the sort of puzzle I like and I'm getting paid to try to solve it! Part of the fun is that I don't know if there is any solution.

I've been working on inventing that measure for a few months. I've had several conversations with one of my bosses, Shiela [sic] Strauss, who knows more math than I do. But I keep playing with it, whenever I don't have something else to do, and it buzzes around in my head even when I'm not at work.

Today, I finally figured it out:

Here it is:

$$Q(x) = \sum_{a=1}^{i} \sum_{b=i+1}^{n-1} g_{ab}(x)/g_{ab}i(j-1)$$

where i and j are the number of nodes in the two sub-networks, $g_{ab}(x)$ is the number of geodesics connecting a and b that include x, and $i(j-1)$ is a scaling factor to make measure range between 0 and 1.

Why is this useful? Well, suppose you have a network of a bunch of people, some of whom have sex with each other and some of whom have HIV. HIV can only spread if one person has it and the other does not. If you want to estimate how fast it will spread through a network, you have to know how much sex is happening between the people who are HIV positive and those who are not.

Figuring this out is fun.

I also get along with a lot of the people I work with. A group of us often go to lunch together. This feels really good. I have a great job!

But, just as I got lost on campus, I get lost getting near work.

The World Trade Center had a lot of entrances and the streets in that neighborhood. it were far from being a grid. Getting to work isn't so bad: As with getting to David's apartment, I memorize a route, verbally. But I go out to lunch and forget which exit leads to which restaurants. And then I have to get back to work from a restaurant. That never gets easy, but if I am with others, I can just go where they go. But how do *they* know? Why don't I? What is wrong with me?

***

After the fiasco with my first dissertation, I want to propose one that won't possibly get turned down, so I go with one that is highly technical and work with one of the most senior professors in the department, John Walsh, who teaches statistics and about 60 years old. I've been his teaching assistant for one semester and, on my evaluation, he crossed out all the questions and just wrote "Super!" in really big letters. He is a very nice man and he is an excellent mentor.

The new dissertation is highly technical. The title, if you really want to know, is *Collinearity Diagnostics in Multiple Regression: A Monte Carlo Study*. Multiple regression is a statistical technique where there is one dependent variable (the thing you want to explain) and a bunch of independent variables (the thing you think will help explain the dependent variable). In psychology and many other fields, the independent variables are often related to each other. For instance, if you are looking at risk of suicide, you might look at measures of anxiety and depression. Those two often go together. This is called collinearity. Sometimes this can cause problems with the regression. There are various ways to try to diagnose problematic collinearity, and, in my dissertation, I plan to compare several of those ways.

Dr. Walsh and I put together a committee and, this time, the proposal goes well. Then, one of my committee members dies of cancer that advanced very rapidly. She is replaced. Then another member is fired after he is caught *in flagrante delicto* with a graduate student in his office. He is replaced. I sail right through the progress report.

So, of the five people who have to approve my dissertation, one is my mentor, I know he will approve. One is the chair of the department. She likes me and feels bad for me about the first dissertation and doesn't really understand what I'm doing, so, she will approve. One is the other remaining member from my original committee. He probably does understand it. The final members are substitutes for the two who left. I'm pretty sure I will succeed. I liked and knew the original committee members; they were appropriate for my dissertation—within psychology they were quants.

I go into the chair's office for the defense. They invite me to sit. My defense is very short. The five of them are sitting there. The department chair asks "Why are your results important for psychology?" and I tell her. She asks "What are your recommendations for practice?" and I say that "people should use condition indexes to diagnose collinearity." Then they ask me to excuse myself.

I go out into the hall. I'm pretty sure I passed. First, almost no one fails their defense. Second, my mentor is the senior member of the department. Thrid, I think the committee feels bad about what happened on my first proposal. But, most important, no one but my mentor understands what I did!

After a few minutes, they ask me to come back in and the chair congratulates me. It feels good, but a little anticlimactic. My committee and my defense was so easy! These professors aren't qualified to judge my dissertation. They filled in for others. Also, unlike most degrees, a class doesn't all graduate at once. I'm the second one done of my group of friends, but that's really happenstance more than anything. But, hey! I'm a doctor!

I call my parents and I call Leslie and they all congratulate me. And I tell my friends at Fordham, who also express their happiness for me.

When I get home, Leslie asks me, teasingly, if I was going to make people call me "Dr. Flom" and I say "No one calls me 'Mr. Flom!"

One issue with us, though, is that she is really bad at math and has no idea what I'm doing at school or at work. When her friends ask her what I do, she says (as she tells me) "some math thing." And it's one big thing we can't talk about. I can't tell her what I do all day. At one conference that I go to, I go out to lunch with some friends and one says "the other day at breakfast I was discussing the DATA STEP [1] with my wife ..." and I wonder what that must be like.

To celebrate getting my Ph.D., I am throwing a party for myself at an Italian restaurant that Leslie and I like. I've invited Leslie, of course, and my parents, some friends and some professors from Fordham, some friends from NDRI, some of the friends of Leslie who I have become close to; altogether about 25 people. I'm looking forward to it, despite being an introvert. I've deliberately picked a relatively calm and quiet restaurant near where we live on the upper west side and where we are known. It's a nice, casual place. Usually I go there in my typical jeans and tee shirt, but tonight I wear a button down shirt and a jacket.

We have three tables. My mom and dad are seated at a table with my mentor, John Walsh, who they had never met, and other people from that generation, including Sam Friedman, my boss at NDRI. Dad is wearing his usual suit. John is in a blazer. I don't know if Sam owns a suit (there are reasons I like him).

Everyone seems to be having a good time. Wine is being poured, meals are being ordered, and there are some snacks on the table. Then I hear my mother tell John "I married an idiot." He looks kind of startled, and my dad, as always, is utterly ignoring her behavior. Even though I'm used to it, it's embarrassing. Maybe I should have warned Dr. Walsh beforehand, but I didn't

---

[1] The DATA STEP is part of every SAS program, and SAS is a computer program that is used for statistical analysis (among other things)

think about it.

***

I first meet Tim Walsh through our wives being pregnant at the same time, Leslie becomes friends with Elana, then Tim and I become friends. Tim introduces me to his brother David and their friend Ken and Bill.

David lives in Greenwich Village which, unlike most of Manhattan, is not on a grid. We often meet at his house, and, when we do, I usually take the 1 train to 14th street. Of course, I get lost the first few times but then I memorize a route, verbally: "Walk to the downtown end of the station, go up the stairs on the right, cross the street, walk two blocks south, then turn a slight left, and walk two more blocks, then cross the avenue." Why can't I find my way around like a normal person?

Sometimes I'm coming from someplace other than my usual and I get there on a different subway, or on a bus, or by walking. Then I get lost. Sometimes, really lost. I can wander for 15 minutes or half an hour, looking and feeling stupid and frustrated.

And Google maps only helps a little.

Chapter 16

My early 40s—Could this be maturity?

For a long time I've wondered what the heck is wrong with me and if it has a name. I know that I am weird, but which weird? I don't fit anywhere, and everyone wants to fit somewhere. I know my symptoms, but I don't know the condition that causes them or even a good label for them. There *must* be *some* other people like me. I mean, there are 8 billion people. Even if I am 1 in a million, there are 8,000 like me. People who can solve quadratic equations but can't make a bed; people who get lost on campus while getting their graduate degrees. But who are they? Where are they?

CHAPTER 16. MY EARLY 40S—COULD THIS BE MATURITY?

I know I am twice-exceptional, or 2E. I've known that since I took the WISC at age 9. But I only know it as symptoms: 60 on one subtest, 160 on another; able to solve quadratic equations, unable to make the bed. According to Google Ngram viewer, the term "twice exceptional" was coined in the early 1980s, but was very, very rare until around 2000, and has been becoming more popular quickly ever since. At some point, I learn it.

I know what I'm good at, I'm good at a lot of the things that we call "smart" or "book smart" or "academically gifted" and that's fine. But is there a name to the deficit E? I know that "minimal brain dysfunction" (the diagnosis I got at age 5) isn't it; in fact, that diagnosis ceased to exist while I was a kid. But none of my therapists and none of my extensive reading about disabilities has revealed any name for what I've got that fits at all well. And my desire to know what is wrong with me spurs or pairs with interest in psychology and measurement more generally. I'm interested in odd and unusual people; I'm particularly interested in profoundly gifted people such as John von Neumann or William James Sidis, even though I'm not nearly that gifted. But I did choose to get a degree in psychometrics.

It's 2000 and I'm 40 years old. Leslie and I have been married for nine years, Gabe is four years old and in preschool. Life is pretty good. We're figuring out where Gabe should go to school—he's clearly different from most kids, but we don't know what it is. On many weekends, we spend some time in Barnes and Noble, looking at books about special needs kids.

But I still don't know what is wrong with *me*.

I pick up *Nonverbal Learning Disabilities: The Syndrome and the Model* by Byron Rourke[1]. First, he studies kids with much higher verbal than performance scores on the WISC. That's me. He notes that many of these kids have problems with tactile perception, visual memory, graphomotor skills, check, check, check. That's me. He also says they have good verbal memory, word decoding, and spelling. This is me, too.

I diagnose myself. I have nonverbal learning disability. This is what's wrong. Now I know and I tell others. Almost no one has heard of it, so I have to explain it when I mention it, but, at last, I have a good label. What a relief! Over the years, I've heard lots of parents (and some kids) complain about labels and about their kids getting labeled. But we get labeled. I've gotten labeled all my life. Lazy, crazy, stupid. A minimally dysfunctional brain. Unmotivated. All sorts of labels! It's so good to have the right one. A self-diagnosis won't help me get funding or services or anything like that, but I don't really want those, I'm all done with school and I'm doing OK at work. It does help me realize that there are others with a lot of my issues.

Of course, it doesn't fit perfectly; psychological diagnoses almost never fit perfectly, but NLD isn't even close to a perfect fit. Rourke says that NLDers are bad at math, while I'm a statistician who has always liked math. He says we are good at rote material, but I am bad at it. He says we are bad at problem solving but, for me, this depends entirely on the type of problem. Finally, he says we have no sense of humor and are bad at math, so it's not a perfect fit! I wonder where I should go to return my sense of humor? And Rourke paints a very negative portrait of NLDers. As a psychometrician, I can tell what is going on. The extreme cases are the ones who are available to him, the ones who define the diagnosis. These are the kids who get seen at clinics or referred

---

[1] I don't remember what made me pick up this book

to psychologists and neuropsychologists. But as an NLDer myself, it pisses me off! It makes it not fit so well. Rourke should know better, or, at a minimum, know that he doesn't know better. That is, he should recognize that, like many physical conditions, NLD (and other LD) aren't dichotomies. Take obesity. You can be a little bit overweight, considerably overweight, or 300 pounds overweight. And that's a simple thing compared to the multifaceted NLD.

Here is a poem I wrote about NVLD that may explain a bit more:

Nonverbal LD

Should I say hello with a handshake or kiss?
How do I know? There are cues that I miss.
Am I standing too close? Am I talking too loud?
Am I causing offense, without knowing how?

Are they laughing at me or with me or what?
Is it teasing or banter? Am I off my nut?
Confining my world to pages and screen
I need no longer look for things I've not seen.

But the real world is still out there.
It still is the place where
Most of our living and loving is done.
And now, who's disabled?
Well, I am, for one.

I think navigating NLD (or any LD) is even worse for 2E people like me. In all sorts of situations, people have told me that I can't be learning disabled. At Emerson and York I was always told I could do better if.... If I applied myself. If I paid attention. If I worked harder. When I was in group therapy, my fellow patients told me, flat out, that I was not learning disabled. I think they meant this as a compliment, sort of, but also with the same sort of "if only" as above. This is a kind of victim blaming. Ut's happened to me in writing groups, where people wonder why I act so weird when I write well, or why I can't write fiction when I can write nonfiction, or why I choose the odd topics that I do.

Bow that I have a name for the deficit "E", I learn more and more about it. I'm good at that, that's part of my good "E" and also part of what I learned in grad school. I read. I browse the internet, which is growing and becoming useful. I learn. I join two Yahoo Groups: NLD-in-common and NLD-Adult. The former is for anyone connected with NLD, including parents and teachers. The latter is only for adults with NLD. These groups are very helpful both to offer ideas on how to cope with NLD and on finding people like me. One thing I read is that a rule for work meetings is to never talk until your boss has spoken. I can do that! I'm bad at knowing when it's my turn to speak, but I'm aware of whether my boss has spoken!

> *It's interesting that, if a person has a lot of trouble with reading, or math, or even a skill such as cooking, we know to break it down into small steps. No one seems to think to do this with tasks that I am bad at.*

I join the Nonverbal Learning Disabilities Association. I start to write and advise about it. This feels really good. Not only have I found a group of people who can relate to my problems, but I am figuring out ways to help them, especially those who are a lot younger than me.

***

Gabe is a baby. Sometimes Leslie gives him a bath and sometimes I do. I make up a song, that I sort of sing to him as I wash him:

I love your little belly
I love your little chest
But your little face
Is the part I love the best.

I love your little neck
And I love your little nose
I love your arms out to your fingers
And your legs out to your toes.

I love you!
Oh yes I do.
I love you!
A boopedo.

I love you

I don't think Dad ever gave me a bath. Mom must have. But I don't remember any bath time songs. On the other hand, I don't remember anything from when I was a baby, so who knows? But I do know I really like being Gabe's dad. I always thought I would, but it's good to have my suspicions confirmed.

***

Gabe is 2 or 3, and we are up at Beechwood. Dad and I are sitting in the foyer under the big staircase. Gabe is playing nearby. Dad turns to me and says "You know, it's interesting. When you were a kid you did this and this and this, and now Gabe does that and that and that". He is accurate. So, I turn to him and say "Dad! So you were paying attention!" and he sort of shrugs.

Mom had always told me he was never home, never paid attention to us, and did nothing. I always knew she exaggerated: We did see him sometimes. I figured she only exaggerated a little. Certainly, he isn't very present in my memories of my early years, and I know he was a workaholic. But here he is, identifying ways I acted as a kid and comparing me to Gabe at the same age.

How did he know? He must have been paying more attention than Mom said, since no one can learn anything without observing. But I think one aspect of his genius was processing information faster than most people, so, he could learn more from less than the rest of us can.

***

Gabe is two. As usual, when I get home from work, Leslie tells me about what happened that day. But today something unusual happened. She had taken him with her to go shopping. He pointed to the sign over the door and said "Exit". She was amazed and now, when she tells me, so am I. We aren't the sort of parents who drill our baby with flash cards. Of course we read to him a lot, from the usual sort of age-appropriate books. He has one bath book about a swan that swims, and there's Dr. Seuss and all that sort of thing; but nothing more than that. We decide to find out what other words he can read and write and there are quite a few. One odd thing is that when he gets a word wrong, he gets it completely wrong; he doesn't get one or two letters off, he reads a completely different word.

Gabe likes to play alone. He likes to be alone in his room. Today he told me "OK, Daddy, you can watch me play, but you

CHAPTER 16. MY EARLY 40S—COULD THIS BE MATURITY?

have to lie on my bed and not talk." I know that isn't how little kids ordinarily relate to their parents!

Gabe age 2

***

Gabe is in preschool. Some days, I wake up early and help him get dressed because I don't mind getting up early and Leslie likes to sleep later. Today, when he comes home, Leslie notices that his sweatpants are on backwards. I must have put them on that way and he hadn't noticed. My boy. The teachers at preschool tell us he always sits and plays by himself. My boy again. This upsets Leslie more than it does me. He doesn't seem unhappy about it; the teachers say he seems content alone, and he shows no signs of misery at home. He just likes playing alone.

***

Gabe is three and a half. We're on the plane home after a family vacation, this time to the Caribbean, courtesy of Dad. Mom, as usual, spent vacation complaining about things, but the rest of us had a good time. On the plane home, I talk to Gabe:

ME: Hey Gabe. Did you have fun on vacation?
GABE: Yes.
ME: Did you have fun with Uncle Jason?
GABE: Yes.
ME: Did you have fun with Aunt Wendy?
GABE: Yes.
ME: And did you have fun with Alison?
GABE: Yes.
ME: And Grandpa?
GABE: Yes.
ME: And did you have fun with Grandma?
GABE: No. She's scary.

Although I know that Mom can be scary, I wonder what a three year old sees scary in her, but it's there, somewhere. I don't say anything to him, but I figure we must have a pretty smart kid on our hands.

***

Gabe is four and playing a Sesame Street game on the computer in our apartment. One of the games asks you to put a face on Elmo, and it has a bunch of different eyes and mouths and so on. You are supposed to make Elmo look happy or sad or whatever. It's the only part of the game that Gabe has trouble with. So I try, I have my own problems, even though I am about 40 years old and have a Ph.D.

Even though I know, for sure, that Gabe is not genetically related to me, I feel some additional connection start growing. The sweatpants, the playing alone, and now, the faces. Of course he's also different. He seems much happier with himself than I was. I learned to read at a normal age and in the usual way, learning to sound things out. I was always active and he is much less so.

CHAPTER 16. MY EARLY 40S—COULD THIS BE MATURITY?

***

Gabe is five and I'm lying with him in bed before he goes to sleep. Either Leslie or I do this each night. We are talking and he says "Today someone called me 'stupid'. I'm not stupid." I agree with him. He didn't say it angrily or shamefully. He wasn't embarrassed, he was puzzled. He couldn't figure out why someone would say something that wasn't true. It was as if someone had said he was purple. I think to myself "if that's how he reacts to insults, then we are doing something very right." Rick once told me that being a parent is the only job where you don't know for 25 years if what you are doing is working. But I'm beginning to think that what we are doing is working very well.

But he is clearly unusual. Even though he learned to read words very early, he still isn't reading sentences. And he acts oddly in many ways. Sometimes he makes motions that are sort of like what martial arts would be if the person didn't know anything about martial arts. I'm much more OK with his oddities than Leslie is, probably because I was so odd as a kid and she was not.

I've just recently diagnosed myself, and now Leslie and I search book after book in Barnes & Noble, looking for one that describes Gabe. We often take him together to the store and one of reads kids' books with him, while the other searches the special education shelves (luckily, the two sections are right next to each other). Today I picked up *The Out of Sync Child*. Like many such books, it has a checklist of symptoms and he has a lot of them; most of them seem to go together: Aversion to noise, dislike of sudden movements; things like that. Then I read "is frequently constipated" and I think we have hit on something. Good to have a diagnosis, or, at least, a start on one!

Many people who find a diagnosis for themselves or their kid get worried. But I figure that the diagnosis doesn't change the person. They still have all the same issues. They've just learned something. That's good.

I figure that we can get the people at Gateway to try to help. I didn't think he would be *going* to Gateway, but, given my relationships to the school, I figure it can't hurt.

Toby Pulanco has been at Gateway since my second year there. I'm one of only five alumni or students who never have her as a teacher. Some people are born to do certain things. Toby was born to teach special ed. She reads kids amazingly quickly, and likes all of them. Once, at an alumni party, she remembers every one who talks to her, even though she hadn't seen some of them in decades and even though some are now taller than she is.

Naturally, Leslie and I have been talking about Gabriel a lot. Mostly, we agree on things. But there is a lot to process. I wonder if my parents talked about me this way, or did Mom just decide what to do and tell Dad? And, even though Mom did start Gateway for me, I have to feel that both Leslie and I are more attuned to Gabe than Mom ever was to me. We aren't as organized or driven as she was; neither of us could have started a school and made it so successful. But Gabe knows he is loved and accpeted in ways that I never did.

***

It's September 11, 2001, I get up early, like usual. I go and vote in the primary election near our apartment. Then I go to the subway stop at 86th and Broadway and take the subway to work. I take the elevator to the 16th floor and go to my cubicle. I order some breakfast. Right after that, I hear something go "thump" as if someone had dropped a big box of paper on the 17th floor, right above my head. Then someone says "The other building is on fire!" and I go look and, sure enough it is. I figure there was some electrical fire, or something shorted out, or whatever. I'm certainly not thinking terrorists, or that our building might be next.

Then our office manager tells us all to evacuate. He's very calm about it, but I've never seen him really excited about anything. The few of us who are there early go down 16 flights of stairs. It's not very crowded or crazy at this point; partly because there aren't a lot of people on floors below me (16 is misleading, as several of the lower floors were lobby); partly because it's early; and partly (as I learn later) because the Port Authority's early statements are not to evacuate.

I'm almost all the way down the stairs. in the lobby or basement level, I feel the building shudder a little.

Now I'm outside. It's rush hour, so it's fairly busy, but not that many people have evacuated yet. But now *both* buildings are on fire. Things are falling. Everyone is speculating wildly. Terrorism? Accidents? 747s? Who knows? Everyone is standing around. But I figure that anything that fell from the buildings could kill me, so I run to a subway (I can't take my usual 1 train, because the station is under the building). When I get to the station, everyone is leaving the subway to go to work. I say "go home, you won't be working today" and they all look at me like I'm crazy. I get on whatever train comes, going north. I get uptown, then take a bus the rest of the way home.

I turn on the TV and watch the buildings collapse, just as people all over the world are doing.

I'm fine. I have some glass in my hair, but I'm not injured. But Leslie has just dropped off Gabriel at Gateway down on 14th street. And I'm thinking about how my parents, and Nancy, and Jason and others can find out I'm fine. Cell phones don't work. How will Gabe get home?

Then I get a call from my father's secretary. Land lines seem to still be working, off and on. She tells Dad and Nancy that I'm

OK, but there's no way to reach Leslie. Hours go by, the TV is endlessly looping the same thing. Davida Sherwood, the director of Gateway, gets Gabe and Leslie (who has gone back to the school) a ride home. They get home around 2 PM. We all go out to dinner at Time Cafe, which is one of our favorite restaurants. It's very strange.

***

Soon after 9/11, Leslie and I decide to have another child. We saved sperm from the same donor. Once again, Leslie gets pregnant on the first try. We soon discover it's going to be another boy. I'm fine with that. I would be fine with a girl, too. It feels to me that saying or thinking "I want a boy" is, in a way, saying "I don't want a girl" and I don't think or feel that. And Leslie says "at least he won't steal my clothes."

This time, choosing a name is a bit easier. We agree that the name should start with E because Leslie's father, Edward Beyer, has died. But we can't agree on which E name. Leslie wants it to be "Ethan" but I argue that "Ethan Flom" sounds too much like that old book. We settle on "Evan."

At the end of June, Leslie goes in for her last pregnancy check up. When she comes home, she tells me that Evan has the cord wrapped around his neck and relays the conversation she had with Dr. Rodke:

DR. R: Well, we could wait for this to be a life threatening emergency over a holiday weekend, but let's not. How about July 2?

LESLIE: Peter's birthday is July 2.

DR. R: OK, let's make it July 3.

Neither of us is too worried; neither of us are big worriers about medical conditions. We had planned a c-section in any case, because of the same concerns as with Gabe, and the doctor did say that we are going to *avoid* a life threatening emergency, not have one!

***

From birth, and even in the womb (according to their mom), Evan and Gabriel are very different boys. In the womb, Evan kicked like most fetuses; Gabe had been so still. In all those *What to Expect* books, Gabe was never doing what he was supposed to be doing. He was doing some things that older kids should be doing, and not doing what his age was supposed to be doing. He was all over the map. Evan was mostly doing things right on target, or a little ahead.

One exception is art, drawing in particular. Evan starts drawing a lot when he is about three. He carries drawing tools everywhere.

As Evan grows up, he does all the normal things and I learn what normal development looks like, firsthand. He makes friends, he gets mad at them, he stops being mad at them. He keeps some friends and not others. All this is new to me! I've read about normal development in my education and psychology classes, but I have no first or second hand experience of it. My childhood was anything but normal; Jason was too close in age for me to be a really good observer when we were young and his adolescent years weren't too normal either.

I think partly as a result of this, and partly because of their shared interest in art, Leslie gets closer to Evan and I get closer to Gabe. Leslie worries more about Gabe than I do, and Evan talks more to her than he does to me.

***

Gabe is 8 and Evan is 2. Evan has learned to talk. And talk he does! One day, when we are all out together, Gabe turns to Evan and says "don't you *ever* stop talking?"

***

Evan is five. Today, he tells Leslie and me that he doesn't feel like talking. This takes him about ten minutes.

***

Another way Gabe and Evan are different is that Gabe is still and Evan moves. For a while, Evan moves around even when he is reading or writing.

***

Gabe is 10 or 11 and I poke my head into his room and say "Hey Gabe, I love you." And he says "Daaaaad ...I *know*." This is a good day. I don't know what we did right. To me, our parenting seems normal. Pay attention to them. Love them. Talk to them and listen to them. Comfort them when they are upset. Sure, Leslie and I have read lots of books on parenting. But most of it just seems normal.

***

It's early autumn, 2007. Gabe is 11 and Evan is 5. The grant money for HIV research dries up after drugs to treat it are developed, and NDRI shrinks a lot, including letting me go. I worked there for a decade so it is something of a shock to leave, but I stay in touch with some of my colleagues for a while. I'm sad to be leaving, as it was a great job with interesting work and nice people. But I'm not particularly worried. I know I don't have to find a job immediately, and I know my skills are valuable.

***

In 2007 I hear about a conference that the NLDA is holding in November in Stamford, Connecticut. I call to get information and and get invited to be a speaker. I'm not sure why, I haven't really done anything public about my diagnosis yet. Maybe they are asking everyone to be a speaker? In any case, I'm excited to be doing it. Unlike most people, I like public speaking.

I make train reservations and a hotel reservation at the conference hotel. I think about what I want to say. The day before the conference I take the train up to Stamford. Like at any conference, people arrive by themselves or in small groups. There's a big conference hall where everything happens. There's a stage in front for the speakers and chairs for the audience. Altogether about 150 people attend.

There are presentations. I sit in the audience for those. One of the earlier ones is from a vendor has presented a tool that is useful for kids with dyslexia and dysgraphia (trouble with writing). It translates pictures into words, so you can try to draw your thoughts. There was a negative reaction to this from all the NLD people in the audience. There was a sort of collective recoil. I raise my hand. The speaker calls on me. I say "Anything that is good for people with dyslexia is probably bad for us. I don't want a tool that turns drawing into writing. I can't draw. If anything, I want a tool that turns writing into drawing." This gets a positive reaction from the crowd. Some laughter, some *sotto voce* agreement, some nods. Most of the other speakers are much better.

In between presentations, I walk around and talk to people. It's great to be among people who have similar issues to me; I've met some of the attendees online. And I see vendors who are interested in NLD. It's great. These are my people, for at least one of my E's.

Now it's my turn to speak. I'm a little bit nervous, but not too much. At this point, I've given lots of talks, but this is my first about NLD. I walk on stage and introduce myself. I speak without any real notes, because I know what I want to say. "Remember that we NLDers have no sense of humor." Then I turn around so my back is to the audience and say, in a monotone, "We are especially bad at sarcasm and tone of voice." There is laughter. I look over my shoulder and smile at the audience. Then I say "It must be true. I read it in a book. By an expert." Even more laughter. Byron Rourke is not too popular with this crowd (I don't actually mention him, as he might be in the audience, but lots of people know who I mean). This is really working!

I turn back around and tell them that, since I have no sense of humor, I made up a variation of a joke.

> A guy is flying in a hot air balloon and he's lost. So he lowers himself down over a field and shouts to a guy on the ground:
>
> BALLOON GUY: Excuse me! Can you tell me where I am and which way I'm headed?
>
> GROUND GUY: Sure! You're at 43 degrees, 127 minutes, 32 seconds north, 99 degrees, 74 minutes, 13 second east. You're at 201.3 meters above sea level and right now you're hovering, but on your way here you were on a vector of 1.879 radians at 2.992 meters per second.
>
> BG: Thanks! By the way, do you have NVLD?
>
> GG: Sheesh! I do! But how the heck did you know that?
>
> BG: Well, everything you told me is accurate, you gave me more detail than I needed, and you told it to me in a way that's no use to me at all!
>
> GG: Huh. Are you a clinical psychologist?
>
> BG: I am! But but ... HOW did you know that?
>
> GG: You don't know where you are and you don't know where you are going. You got where you are by blowing hot air. You like to stick

labels on people after asking them a few questions. And you're in exactly the same position you were a few minutes ago only now, somehow, it's my fault!

But remember, we have no sense of humor.

As the joke goes on, there is more and more laughter. By the end, a lot of people are hysterical, which also feels great. It's nice to get people to laugh at you on purpose.

I go on to talk about diagnoses in general. I say "No diagnosis fits me perfectly, nor, likely does it fit any of you perfectly. But labels can be useful. They can help you get services, they can help you find community, they can make you feel less alone. But they can become boxes and, while labels can be useful, boxes are for groceries." When I finish there is lots of applause and, throughout the rest of the conference people tell me about it and tell me how great my talk was. I hear from NLDers themselves, their parents, and their teachers. The NLDers are glad to hear from one of their own, the parents and teachers are glad to learn about ways to help.

This conference was a great experience for me. Now, I am not just an adult, but I am mature enough to talk sensibly and openly about what is wrong with me. It feels great to deliberately make the audience laugh, but I've been funny for a long time. What feels even better is that I'm helping people.

Chapter 17

My 50s and 60s

It's 2007 [1]. Gabe is 11 and Evan is 5. I decide to do some more writing. I find a company called Gotham Wirters' Workshops that has classes right in New York City. I take a class in creative non-fiction. It's a really good class and it spurs me to work some more on a book I've been thinking about, off and on, for a long time, about being learning disabled.

***

It's Thanksgiving, 2007 and, after a long battle with various cancers (which I learned about very piecemeal and sometimes not at all), my mother is in New York Hospital and is near death. Even in the hospital, she clipped newspaper articles for me. I don't know which cancers she had when, or what the first one was. She gives me only fragmentary information and doesn't answer questions about it. Maybe she's been telling my dad or Nancy, I don't know.

Although it's clear she's dying in the next few days, Dad takes Nancy and Jason and me and our wives and kids out to a restaurant near the hospital for Thanksgiving dinner. At one point, he turns to me and says "I'm 83 years old, I'm single, and I'm rich" and shrugs his shoulders. I don't say anything. I don't think anyone

---

[1] OK, technically, I'm not quite 50

else hears what he says. It's such a Joe Flom thing to say. Who says such a thing at a time like this, after 49 years of marriage? It's not exactly accurate because Mom is still alive, and it seems wrong. People who are close to him and know him well can tell he is devastated. But he would never express that, at least, not to me.

Then we have Thanksgiving dinner.

That Saturday night I am home with Leslie and the boys. The phone rings. It's Nancy. Mom has died. I feel a kind of relief that she is no longer suffering, but I don't feel any accompanying grief.

We are holding shiva of sorts for her at their apartment, even though none of us are remotely religious. We are all standing around, eating and drinking, and talking about Mom and other things.

Across the room I see some woman hit on Dad, right there during the shiva. He seems to be ignoring her, or maybe he is oblivious. I knew he would be a great catch, but I didn't think it would happen quite this soon.

Later, I'm talking to my cousin Stuart and Nancy a lot. I find out that the career my mother always said she gave up when she had me was not any big thing. She had only been a decorator for a few years. This comes as something of a revelation. I had figured out, ages ago, that a lot of what my mother said was nonsense, but I never thought she would have lied about something like this. But, thinking about it, she didn't actually lie. She never *said* how long she had been a decorator, but she made a big deal of it. I inferred that she had been a decorator for a long time. But she wasn't. She started it after Nancy got old enough not to require a lot of supervision.

I also find out that she lied about my father's father. From listening to her, Itzig Flom sounded like a primitive who wasn't very smart and was stuck back in the old country in some ways. Stuart tells me that Dad got his brains from his own father and that Itzig was kind and considerate and nice to Stuart.

Neither Nancy nor I speak at her memorial. There is nothing either of us wants to say that would be appropriate and I'm not willing to compromise my feelings by blathering things I don't think. Jason does speak. Jason's relationship with her was fundamentally different from ours, from birth right on through childhood, and all of his life right up to her death, he is also very good at this sort of speech.

Mom's gone, but I'm not grieving . I don't feel anything like that.

I envy people who miss their mothers after they die.

***

After 50 years of marriage, Dad doesn't know how to be single. He eats almost every meal in restaurants, he pays people to clean. But there's so much else he can't do.

He gets married again in about a year. How many 50 year old people get to be the son of the groom? I'm fine with him marrying so soon. Leslie is less so, she thinks it is inappropriate or even disrespectful. I understand her points, but I realize he just needs to be married. His new wife is nice enough. She's around 25 years younger than he is (he is 84 at this point) and gets him doing things he's never done before. At their engagement party, I tell the Ben Gurion joke about heaven and hell that I had learned in Israel and it breaks up the crowd.

***

My marriage is continuing its long slide into a sort of "roommates who share kids" state. It's a weird feeling. I know people who love their spouses and stay married forever; I know people who are so out of love with their spouses that divorce is obviously needed. This isn't either of those, it's just sort of blah. However, the kids are doing fine. Gabe is 12 and is doing fine at Gateway. Evan is 6 and is at the local public school. We thought about putting Evan in a private school but decided against it; Leslie was more against it, I was more in favor, but she convinced me.

***

After leaving NDRI I had a few other jobs; in May, 2010, I became a consultant.

***

It's 2008 and I see a book at Barnes & Noble: *Outliers: The Story of Success* by Malcolm Gladwell. It looks interesting so I buy it. Chapter 1 is about the world's best hockey players. Chapter 2 is about the 10,000 hour rule, The Beatles, Bill Joy (sometimes called "the Edison of the internet"), Bill Gates, Steve Jobs, and Paul Allen. Chapter 3 is about how IQ only matters up to a point and Christopher Langan (one of the highest IQ people ever). Chapter 4 is more about Langan, and also Robert Oppenheimer (the "father of the atom bomb"). And, there in chapter 5 is Joe Flom! Of course he didn't tell me he was the focus of a whole chapter of a book that is on the best seller lists. And I read that chapter with particular interest. I don't really learn anything new about Dad, but it's something to see it in print.

Next time I see Dad, I mention that I read about him in a book, he tells me the book got everything wrong.

***

It's December 26, 2010, four and a half years after my mom died. Dad is in the hospital for heart surgery in the middle of a blizzard. Jason and Nancy and I are going to visit him. The streets are covered in sheets of ice, because the sanitation department messed up, and partly because it was Christmas. Getting to the hospital is quite an adventure for Jason and Nancy and me, but we do make it. Dad does come home for a bit. But he never really recovers and is mostly in the hospital until he dies on February 23, 2011. My brother and I spend a lot of time at the hospital, talking to him or to each other, or even just sitting.

Dad gets obituaries in, among other places, *The New York Times* and *The Washington Post*. I write one, albeit a bit prematurely, on Daily Kos. It got copied in *Above the Law*. I read all of these but somewhat clinically. I don't learn anything new from reading them. I'm curious as to where he gets obituaries and how big they will be.

We decide to wait until Spring to have a memorial service. People at his law firm do most of the organizing, with a lot of help from my sister. They book Alice Tully Hall at Lincoln Center. Jason and I discuss who should speak when. We agree that he will go first, then partners and clients and colleagues, and then me.

Now I have to write something! I think about it off and on and write it mostly in my head, but I do make notes. They are five words long.

***

It's the day of Dad's memorial. I dress in a suit and Leslie dresses up too. Before we head out, Leslie checks that my tie is knotted correctly and that I haven't gotten my shirt buttoned wrong (I do that a lot, and I haven't worn a button down shirt in a while). We take a cab to Lincoln Center and I finalize my speech on the way to the service.

We go in and find our seats near the front. Alice Tully Hall seats over 1,000 people and it's getting pretty full. As we arranged, Jason goes first. He does fine. Among the other speakers are Don Drapkin (a client), Roger Aaron (a partner), and Susan Plum (director of the Skadden Fellowship) [2] speak. I find out something I didn't know. People mention that his highest praise of them was to yell at them, because he only did that if he thought they could learn

---

[2]The Skadden fellowship is a program that Dad spearheaded, where law school students who are interested in public interest law apply and, if they win, get two year fellowships

from it. And I find out he was fond of writing very short, cryptic, comments on their work. This, they say, was a compliment. When I hear this, it makes me remember the note Gershon put on my paper, all those years ago, and feel better about it.

Then it's my turn. I walk to the podium and look out at a sea of faces. It's the biggest audience I've had.

I start by saying that "I am not going to talk about Dad at work. I am going to talk about him as father." There is some laughter already. Good. Then I say that he lived a long life, which was surprising for two reasons and a good thing for two reasons.

"It's surprising", I say "not only because for the first half of it, he had been very overweight, a big drinker, a workaholic, and a cigar smoker but also because, when I was three and Jason was two, he took us both to the beach. There was no life guard. He fell asleep. And, when he came home, he told Mom and she didn't kill him." Lots more laughter.

"It was also a good thing for two reasons", I continue. "One is that I got to know him as an adult and the other is that he got to know his grandchildren, who he spent a lot more time with than he ever did with us." Then I mention that when I was five years old he got me a typewriter for my birthday and that when I was at camp I got a letter from him signed "sincerely, Joe". Laughter keeps building Then I say "and that's all I got." There is a lot of applause. That feels good.

It was a good speech. It got lots of compliments, both at the event and my phone call and e-mail. People stop me on the street for a long time afterward to say what a great speech it was. Jason tells me I should do stand up (and he does stand up, sometimes).

But, looking back, I wish I had closed by talking about that note from Gershon, and then saying "There's a problem here. No one has a glass of champagne. It's time to fix this."

***

Nancy moved back to New York a few years ago to run a foundation my parents had set up and to help take care of them as they aged. We go out for lunch together every once in a while, usually at the Viand Cafe on 75th and Broadway.

I am about 50 years old and I've figured out that Nancy might not know that she had saved my life when I was suicidal as a tween and teen. Back then, I assumed she knew; I was pretty self-centered and unaware. That assumption has just sort of lasted, but has been under assault as I've grown up and started being more of a whole person. For her not to know this is intolerable. She has to know and I have to tell her. So, I call her up to have lunch at our usual spot.

She is there before me, sitting in a booth facing the entrance. We greet eachg other and hug and then, after the usual catching up I tell her, "You know, you saved my life, right?" "What?" she says, looking surprised.

So, I tell her that I would have killed myself if it wasn't for her. It had been so vital to have someone else who saw Mom the way I saw her — no one else who knew her saw her as anything less than wonderful (well, I'm guessing all the people she fired over the years would not speak well of her, but her friends all did). And I tell her that I wish I had taken her up on her offer for me to move in with her and Rick when I was a teen.

She is amazed. She surely knew that I was not a happy teenager but she didn't know I had been suicidal. And she certainly didn't know I had sat on a ledge, even now, I didn't tell her that. Most of all, she hadn't known how important she had been to me.

She was amazed. She was flabbergasted. But, most of all, she was glad. And I was very glad to have told her.

***

We go on trips as a family, often to some big city, since neither Leslie nor I drive. One thing this brings to mind is how lucky I am to be living in Manhattan, with its grid arrangement of numbered streets. I get lost everywhere. But, on a trip to London in 2012, when Evan is 10, it turns out that he has a really good sense of direction. Our hotel is on a tiny street that even some city guides haven't heard of. But, after one day in the city, Evan can tell us how to get there, just by looking at landmarks.

***

Nancy is 66 years old and, while we are sitting in the back seat of a cab she tells me and Leslie that she has non-Hodgkin's lymphoma and that it can't be treated very well. I ask what I can do and she tells me there isn't anything to do and that she doesn't want to talk about it. This is very Nancy-like. She doesn't know how to be the one who needs help and she found a way to tell us where we wouldn't hug her or anything. Who can hug in the back of a cab?

She gets sicker and sicker. She was already thin, but she gets thinner. Leslie volunteers to help in any way, such as picking up groceries from the store, but Nancy refuses. But whenever we talk on the phone and I ask how she is, she will say something like "I'm terrible, let's not talk about it."

I don't have any idea how to get around this and offer help in a way that she would accept. She's *Nancy*. She's my big sister. How do we switch to being two adults? How do I tell her that I'm now an adult and can help? Maybe some neurotypical little brother could figure it out, but I can't.

Toward the end, she refuses visitors other than her sons. She says she doesn't want us to see her the way she is now. She dies of cancer on January 24, 2015. Because of her long illness, I was prepared for her death. I was very glad, again, that I had told her she saved me. And I was sorry, again, that we had never really figured out how to be adults together.

Nancy's sons Aaron and Jonathan decide to wait to have a memorial service. I fly to Chicago for the event.

So many people have warm things to say. It was a very informal get together, but a reminder of how good a person she was and more notice to me that she had had such a big effect, not just on me and her kids, but many others. I'm glad they waited to have this memorial; it works better now than it would have right after her death.

***

Early in 2016, I finally publish my book. It's called *Screwed Up somehow but not Stupid: Life with a Learning Disability*. I decide to self-publish after learning that, if you go with a publisher, the author only gets about 10% of the retail price, but, if you self-publish, you get about 90%. I look into one publisher that does this kind of book, but I hear that they don't do much in the way of promotion, so I decide I will be better off self-publishing.

***

It's September, 2017. Gotham Writers Workshop, where I took a class back in 2006, also has something called Friday Night Write-in, where you come to their office and sit in rooms. Each room fits about 15 people. The teacher gives a writing prompt and everyone writes. Then, if you want, you can share what you wrote. There's a break with wine and snacks and then you do it again.

One night, a guy named Billy asks me to go out for drinks with a group he has put together. We become friends and we often go out after the write-in and have dinner and/or drinks. But things are going on that I'm only dimly aware of: There's flirtation, there are relationships, there are declined relationships. Most of this I only learn about when other people tell me.

***

I am about 55 years old and decide to find a new therapist. Mostly, I am worried about relationships, both friendly and romantic. I still haven't figured out friendship and, while I do have a couple friends, it doesn't feel like enough. And my marriage isn't very satisfying.

I ask my son's therapist and he gives me two names. One is a block and a half from me, the other is 10 blocks away, so I start with the nearer one. I start seeing her and it's okay, but she is too insistent that there is nothing wrong with me when I know there is. Why can no one see that I am screwed up? Why can't I explain it? After a lifetime, I know *some* of the reasons:

- It's a learning disability and, even in the 21st century, even people who *know* about learning disabilities don't always *believe* in them.

- It's a weird LD that doesn't match with what most people think of as LD. It's not about reading, it's not about math. It's about stuff that most people learn automatically.

- My abilities mask it, to a degree. Many people, even some therapists, don't really believe that a person can be 2E.

And she wants to see me more than once a week, which seems off, especially if she thinks there is nothing wrong. The last straw, though, is that one day I call to cancel, well in advance of a session, because I will be out of town. She insists that I pay or reschedule.

So, off to the one who is farther away.

The new therapist is Gabrielle K and we seem to hit it off right away.

I've been seeing Gabrielle for a few months, and she is a very good therapist. But, even with her, it's hard to get across exactly what is wrong with me. I think therapists have a natural tendency to downplay anything that looks like "wrong" in their patients. And it's even harder when what is wrong is so unusual and nebulous. Another problem is that the setting of therapy is one where my disabilities don't show up. I do well in situations where there are clear social rules. In therapy, I sit in one chair, she sits in the other. We don't switch chairs. She asks about me, but I do very little asking about her. We don't touch. Any notion of romance is prohibited. There's only two of us. And, no matter what I say, it can't be "wrong". Finally, it is a very verbal relationship and I'm good at those.

In more normal interactions, there are also rules, but they are tacit. Breaking them is definitely wrong. And there are rules about *everything*. How close should I be to the other person? How often should I speak? When should I speak? How loudly? What clothing should I wear? Where should I sit (if at all)?

A lot my problems come when I violate these tacit rules. But I can't tell Gabrielle about it because I don't know what rule I have broken. I can recall some of the words spoken, but that's not where the problem is. When I tell Gabrielle what I said, she says things like "that sounds perfect." But the problem isn't what I'm saying.

It's not only that my actions are wrong, it's also that my perceptions are wrong or, more often, lacking. People have expressions and tones of voice and body language and so on and on all the time. They expect you to interpret them. If you know them well, they expect you to interpret them well. And I don't.

Essentially, I'm bad at anything you *didn't* learn at school, that you *weren't* taught, that you just, somehow, got.

After I've been in therapy with Gabrielle for quite a while, she points out that my father was very passive aggressive with my mom, all those years. Every so often, she comes up with something new to me that hits right away, and this is one of those times.

Right away, I think that this would explain a lot of his behavior! After falling asleep at the beach with us babies, she never asked him to take us to the beach again. I wonder, did he even fall asleep? When he unloaded the dishwasher the way he did, did he intend to infuriate her and never be asked to do that again? Then there was the time he took us kids to the supermarket and came back with everything we wanted and very little that was on the list Mom gave him. And, the biggest thing, is how he ignored her nagging for all the years of their marriage. He never defended himself. He never corrected her when she said he did nothing for us as kids. He never defended his father when she insulted him. Nothing.

Still, I wonder. Was it all intentional or was that just how he was and who he was?

***

People think they are being kind by denying that something is wrong; they may even think they are paying compliments. But they aren't. Some therapists seem especially prone to this. They say things like

- "You can't be learning disabled, you're so smart." (A newborn baby can suck and pee and that's about it. Everything else that you can do is learned, and you can be LD in any of it.)

- "You can't be LD and good at reading and math." (What about all the other things people learn?)

- "You can't be gifted and learning disabled". (Why not? Can you be tall and thin?"

***

In December, 2019 I decide to retire. This is a pretty easy decision. My consulting business isn't making much money, I can live without it. And my clients are a pain in the neck a lot. It's just not worth the aggravation.

***

One thing I've been discussing with Gabrielle is my marriage. I tell her how little pleasure I'm getting out of it (and that it seems Leslie isn't getting much, either). After a while, I bring up whether I should get divorced from Leslie. The marriage has gradually gotten less and less good. It never gets really bad; it's not like some couples I hear about where the partners are screaming at each other, or throwing things at each other, or anything like that. We just aren't enjoying each other's company. We aren't doing things together. Even when we have dinner together, we sit in silence unless there is something to talk about with the kids or about the kids.

We do wind up getting very amicably divorced.

Another thing I discuss with her is what I want in a relationship, what I would bring to one, and why I have had so few. I find that I want empathy, even though I have trouble supplying it. But I want empathy of a particular kind. I want recognition. When I tell my inamorata about something that sucked in my childhood, or that there is something I still can't do, or anything like that, sometimes I want her to say "that must suck" and mean it. Because sometimes, life sucks. And, if she wants empathy from me (which I hope she does) then she has to know how to get it. She will have to ask. In words.

So far, I haven't found anyone who can do all this. The women in all three of my serious relationships did *some* of it. You don't have to go out with me for very long (much less stay married for a quarter century!) to realize something is off. And Ronit, Ellen, and Leslie all attempted to do what they could. But it seems to be very rare to be able to supply what I need.

That's one reason I get along with little kids: They tell you what they want, and they are blatant about it.

Chapter 18

Now

Gabrielle tells me that I'm dealing with COVID best of all her patients, relatives, and friends. I like social distancing! I was social distancing when social distancing wasn't cool. I like staying home. I frequently stayed home all day long all my life. People aren't hugging me, which is great. I don't have to wonder if I was supposed to shake hands or hug or what—make as little contact as possible! That's my kind of restriction!

And, during and after the pandemic, I'm actually *more* social than ever before in my life. Nowadays, my evenings are busy! Monday nights I play bridge. Alternate Tuesdays, I meet with one writing group. Most Wednesdays I have a writing class. On many Thursdays I have a meeting of the Broadway Democrats, or more bridge. And, although it's stopped now, for a long time, on Fridays, I was part of Drinking with Atheists This is a great group of people. They have been meeting every Friday evening for many years. Most of them are interesting and intelligent, but, other than that, there is no common thread, other than none of us believe in God. There are men and women; some are gay, some straight; all races; ages from 20s up to 80s; we have philosophy professors and financial advisers and students and a retired nurse and industrial photographers and so on. Pretty much all of us like to talk, but some of the drinking is water.

And it's all online!

I like online!

Online, it's much easier to be social. Not just because I don't have to get dressed and travel (everybody has that) but because, for me, Zoom is good and so is e-mail. Zoom sharply limits the amount of nonverbal language you have to get. Sure, there is still facial expression and tone of voice and related things, but no need to interpret body language, or proxemics (how close you stand to others), or objictics (what clothes you wear and objects you own or display), or many other aspects of nonverbal communication. E-mail removes all the nonverbal stuff: It's just text. Neurotypical people don't like this, because they lose all the nonverbal parts of communication, but, since I get very little of that, I lose much less than they do.

It's not all online, though. David, Ken, Tim, Bill and I are celebrating out tradition of going out, once or twice a year, for a big meal of meat. We are at a steakhouse in Queens. The people at the next table say "You've known each other a long time, right?" and, after thinking about it, I realize I have known them for 25 years, and I'm the newbie!

This brings to mind the fact that, unlike a lot of people, I don't have earlier friends. I have, of course, known Sabha all her life (more than half a century, now) but that relationship is more like siblinghood than friendship. Even within that, it's close but distant because she is in Ireland and has been for almost 50 years. We once visited Ireland and stayed in their house, the last time she visited America she stayed in my apartment. But she is far away.

I don't have any friends from childhood or adolescence or even college. It took me a long time to figure friendship out, and I still haven't got it completely, but at least I am making some new friends now. Better late than never!

I am 64 years old. Some things are still the same and some have changed:

- I no longer call adults that I meet by their last names.

- I haven't stopped writing poems. Some are silly, but my latest serious one is:

Their Presence is a Comfort

> I need a window to jump out of
> A knife to cut myself with.
> I won't use them if They are available. But
> Their presence is a comfort.
> I need a friend to talk to
> A lover to comfort myself with
> I won't abuse them if I could have them. But
> Their presence would be a comfort.
> I need my kids to be dad of
> Their Mom to help out with that.
> I won't cling to them as
> They become men.But
> Their presence is a comfort.

- I still get lost all the time.

- I still can't draw at all.

- I still can't clap in time to music. So I don't try.

- I still don't nap. I've never figured out how. If I do sleep for less than four hours at a time, I wake up confused and tired.

- I still have sleep problems, although, these days, it's more waking up too early than not being able to get to sleep.

- I still don't understand modern art (also, not dance).

- I no longer cry about emotional things, the last time was when I got lost on the way to school in sixth grade. I have no idea why. But I write a poem at some point:

Tricks

> My mind plays tricks on me
> Hiding my emotions
> In a rational sea.
>
> My mind plays tricks on me and
> Searching for a rhyme I find
> A tear has stained the page

- I still think math is beautiful. Last night, I woke up in the middle of the night and thought about when $x^a = ax$ in the dark.

- I still often don't know what is going on around me, socially.

- I still pick scissors up the wrong way, about half the time.

- I still have no sense of when things happened. Not little things, but big ones. What year did my sister get married? Was Gabe born before or after I got my PhD?

- I still don't drive.

- My walls are still white and there is very little art on them.

- I no longer think I am lazy, crazy, or stupid. Well, hardly ever.

- I still have trouble distinguishing good natured teasing from insults.

- I am still weird. Twice as weird.

When I was 15 I knew I would never be whole. I was wrong.

Way back when I was a kid I decided I could be a better dad than my dad was. I think I am. I also think I am a better parent than my mom was. I win. Now what?

Part IV

Appendices

Appendices

In these appendices I cover some topics in more depth than I could in the main text and I also have some bits of advice for other people who are 2E or NLD, or their parents, and also some general thoughts.

Appendix A

Big school, small school, home school

When trying to find a good school for a child with learning disabilities (particularly NVLD), one decision is mainstream vs. special education. I talked about that in an earlier post: Drowning in the Mainstream. But another decision, particularly if you decide against special education, is the size of the school. Clearly, schools vary in size across a huge range, but we can talk, in general, about big schools and small schools. Then there's the smallest school of all: Home school.

Each of these will be right for different children, or even for the same child at different ages. Here are my thoughts on the advantages and disadvantages of each.

Small schools are probably what comes first to mind when considering a placement. The advantages are fairly clear: Your child may receive more individual attention; a higher proportion of the staff will know your child well; any problems that arise may be identified more quickly. The disadvantages may be less obvious, at least to people who are not themselves LD or not expert in LD: That individual attention may also come from other children (and in not so welcome ways). In addition, especially in a small mainstream school, your child may become 'the weird one'. There may be few (or no) other kids with similar issues. NLD children (and other children in the autism ballpark) often have unusual interests—in a small school, it will be less likely that other children share those interests.

Large schools have almost opposite advantages and disadvantages. If the school is not very well run (and, given the student-staff ratios at many schools, it is hard to run a school well) your child may fall between the cracks and be ignored. On the other hand, in a large student body there will be more children who are comparable to your child, both in terms of disabilities and interests.

Then there's home school. I know relatively about this, but it seems to me to offer some unique advantages and disadvantages. The biggest advantages would be knowledge of your child and flexibility of program. The disadvantages (in addition to practical issues of cost and finding materials and instructors and so on) would, I think, be around finding friends.

None of these advantages and disadvantages are set in stone. There are good big schools that manage to track every child well; there are small schools that make huge efforts to find a cohort for each child; and homeschooling can work very well, as well.

How does this play out for choosing a place for your child?

I think that (again, in general) younger children (perhaps up to 4th or 5th grade or so) do better in smaller schools and the older your child gets, the more the advantages of larger places come up.

If your child's issues are primarily social, a larger school (or home school) might be better. If they are primarily academic, a smaller school might be. If your child is good at self-advocating then some of the disadvantages of large schools will become less severe; similarly, if your child fits well into a well-known diagnosis, some of the problems of large schools are less. If your child has multiple issues, is twice exceptional, has very unusual interests, then a small school or home school might be best.

But, again, your mileage may vary. You know your child, I

don't.

Appendix B

Stages of Acceptance

There are, I think, four stages of acceptance of NLD or any disability:

1. There's nothing wrong with me. There must be something wrong with you!

2. There's something wrong with me. Life stinks.

3. There's something wrong with me. You deal with it.

4. There's something wrong with me. I better deal with it.

For short (and for the sake of alliteration), I call these stages denial, depression, display, and dealing. I doubt anyone spends all their time at stage 4; but I think they would be happier if they could spend more time there. I know I would.

Stage 1: Denial

We start off denying difficulties. There can't be anything wrong with me! If there's a problem, it must be something to do with you, or, in a slightly more sophisticated version, with the world. This is, I think, a carryover from infancy and early childhood. A sort of stage 1 is normal for babies, it isn't even conscious. Babies are egotists. Young children often accept themselves as they are at a primitive level, and any fault must lie elsewhere. Newborns are not very capable; it doesn't take much parenting skill to recognize this and attempt to deal with it. But, for disabled kids, as we get older, we (and our parents and siblings and others) start to see a disability—something that normal kids do that we don't. And many of us LD kids keep the earlier attitude: The problem is not with us, but with everyone else.

In older kids or adults this attitude is both less normal and less attractive than it is in little kids. Babies and young kids are natural egotists. They want you to look at them, play with them, and talk to them. They naturally believe that their utterances are interesting, that they are adorable. They are right! Babies are adorable. That's what "cute" means. Further, good parents arrange their world so that not too much can go wrong for their babies and little kids. They provide food and a safe environment. Parents don't allow babies to crawl on windowsills or play alone in the tub. Babies don't have to "do as they are told" because adults know that babies don't understand language ... yet.

Later in childhood, parents and teachers expect kids to take turns in a conversation, ask about others' feelings, and interact appropriately with kids and adults. They also expect kids to start realizing that they make mistakes. As kids age, Stage 1 becomes less and less acceptable and most kids start to use it less and less. Of course, even adults can find themselves in stage 1 sometimes, especially if they are under a lot of stress, or very tired. But older kids and adults who spend a lot of time in stage 1 are not well-regarded.

But if you look at the ways most kids learn to how to interact, it's not surprising that I had trouble learning. My only good relationships were with my sister, my brother, Sabha, and my therapist. Of these, only my brother was even roughly my age. My sister was wonderful, but I couldn't learn to be a kid by watching her, since I never knew her when she was a kid. Sabha was also wonderful, but there was the opposite problem—when I was a kid, she was a baby. You can't learn to be a 7-year-old from a 2-year-old.

I stayed at this stage pretty much all the time until about age 12. Since then, I've gradually spent less and less time there. Now, I spend almost no time there. Ironically, other people nowadays try to tell me there's nothing wrong with me.

Stage 2: Depression

In stage 2, we realize something is wrong, but believe that things will never improve, that there is no way to cope with the difficulty, and that no one else shared this difficulty. For me, this started happening around 4th grade, when I switched to a mainstream school. I could now see NT kids in action. And I wasn't in that action. And I didn't act in those ways. Kids were making friends and I mostly wasn't. I'm guessing that kids started wearing clothes they chose, instead of what their moms chose, but I didn't notice, much less engage. And, while I certainly acted out in class, I didn't do so in peer-acceptable ways. I was jumping to answers, not waiting to be called on, and showing off that I knew stuff. This wasn't what the other kids were doing, but, again, I didn't know what they were doing, much less know how to do it.

And no one really understood this. Even Nancy and Dr. Weintrob didn't. Even now, writing this, it's hard to explain. A blind person misses all the things that come through sight; it's hard to imagine being blind, but we at least have an idea of what we see. Closing our eyes doesn't make us like blind people in any real sense, but it at least shows us what we miss. But the stuff I'm missing is stuff that happens in your brain, not your eyes or ears or fingers.

This lack of understanding probably underlies a lot of my suicidality at this and later stages of my life. During my tweens and teens, it was exacerbated by life events, as I describe in the main text. I didn't know what was wrong and no one else did, either.

There wasn't even a name for what was wrong. No one knew what I was missing out on, because most of what I was missing is absorbed unconsciously by most people.

I was at this stage fairly consistently from age 12 to age 22, but the depth of my stage 2-ness gradually lessened.

Stage 3: Display

In stage 3, we remain aware of our difficulties, and we begin to acknowledge that they might be fixable, but we think it is, largely the responsibility of other people to cope with them, especially after we have told those people about them. The display stage also illustrates another NLD-related problem: determining levels of friendship. Neurotypical people (NTers) move from casual acquaintance to deep friendship gradually, following a series of steps in which more trust is earned and awarded. NTers have many more acquaintances than close friends. Nonverbal cues aid them in moving along this path. How does a person's face look, and how does their voice sound, and what body language are they using, when they talk to you? These are vital cues to levels of friendship, and they are very hard for me and many other NLDers to understand. People do not say, in words, "I'd like to be your acquaintance, but I really don't want to be your friend" or "I enjoy hanging out with you once in a while, but not all the time." Rather they say these things through tone, body language, and facial expression. How do they do this? I don't know! Can I give an example? No, I can't! If I knew how this was done, it would be much less of a problem. And I could then give an example. NT people know how this is done, but it is mostly known at a subconscious level. You do it. But you do it without thought. If you examine your behaviors carefully, you might be able to tell me how you do it.

Similarly, most NTers want to be polite, so they don't say "no" when asked a direct question. They don't say "you are being rude" when they think I'm being rude. They also do not understand that

I do not understand body language and so on. In fact, they are likely unaware of how they read and give nonverbal cues. So, when I misunderstand NTers, they may not be able to explain what cues they were giving. If you misunderstand a word, you can look the meaning up later or ask someone what it means. This is not an option when you misunderstand (or completely miss) nonverbal communication. A further problem is that all of these things are in constant motion.

I entered stage 3 when I was a counsellor at Ramapo. I was at this stage a lot until I moved to Israel, where it gradually diminished.

Stage 4: Dealing

In stage 4, we accept our disabilities and also know that it is primarily our responsibility to cope with them. We also can accept ourselves enough to display without excessive demands. Stage 4 is the only mature stage, and it is by far the most effective stage for having a successful life. As I said, though, few people, if any, manage to stay at this stage all the time. But, then, NT people, even mature, sensible, well-adjusted NT people, don't act maturely all the time, either.

The extent to which you (or the NLDer in your life) can reach and stay at Stage 4 will, I think, have a huge impact on life and happiness. But I haven't figured out the secrets of doing so.

I first got into stage 4 when I was in Israel and, once I got married, I started spending more time there.

Appendix C

Disability as a Mountain

A disability is like a mountain between where you are and where you want to go. There are, I think, four types of responses to this mountain:

1. You can give up, and pretend or decide you don't want to get to the other side of the mountain.

2. You can go over the mountain. I think of this as taking extra time to get to the other side.

3. You can go through the mountain. This is making more effort to get to the other side.

4. You can go around the mountain. This is figuring out some path that neurotypical people often miss or don't even look for.

Each of these has its place.

Well-meaning people too often ignore the first option and the fourth.

You almost never hear anyone tell anyone to give up, unless they are being nasty. But giving up can be the best option. It's almost heretical! We hear "you can do anything you want!" No. You can't. No one can. If you are short, slow, and uncoordinated, you will never have a career as a professional basketball player. We all know this, but we ignore it. For disabled people, there is a bigger list of things we can't do. It's OK, even good, to recognize those things. But, at the same time, we have to recognize what we can do.

Yes, there are exceptions. You can find examples of one-armed baseball players and so on. But those are really, really odd cases. They are fascinating, but they ought not be seen as role models. I mean, do you NT people want to be compared to Albert Einstein, Michael Jordan, and so on? No. You don't. So, if you make an honest effort at something, and don't have any success, maybe you should try something else.

The second and third options are very related to each other, and are the options that are most often recommended. And they can be good. But, before picking one of those, you should think carefully about option four. Abraham Lincoln once said "If I had six hours to chop down a tree, I would spend four of them sharpening my axe." So, before you start whacking at the tree, sharpen your axe. Once your axe is sharp, you may not need more time or effort. But, if you do need more time or effort, you should decide how much, and whether they are worth the reward.

The final option is almost never mentioned by neurotypical adults, but I think it can be the best one in many situations. Find another way, a trick, a work around. What these tricks are depends on you, both your disability and your abilities. One that I use is to note that, in Manhattan, where I live, the numbers of buildings on side streets follow a pattern: Odd numbers are on the north side of the street and even numbers on the south. So, if I come out of a building with an odd number, I know I'm on the north side and am facing south. I have lots more tricks in my first book: *Screwed Up Somehow but not Stupid*.

The reason neurotypical people don't think about this method is that they don't need it and they don't see the mountain that we face. When they recommend more effort or more time, they don't realize how much more time and effort would be involved. For instance, most people can walk along a street, go into a store, come out and just know which way to walk. I can't. So, I made up a trick. I tell myself which way to walk when I enter. I will say to myself "Turn left when you leave." Then I can remember.

Appendix D

Nomenclature

Why "disabled" and not "differently abled"?

The short answer is that everyone is differently abled. Some people are similarly abled, but no two people are identically abled. By putting me into that group of "differently abled" (every human on the planet), you are demeaning me, minimizing my difficulties, and not helping.

I realize that the vast majority of people who use the term "differently abled" don't intend to do that at all. Rather the opposite. They are trying to make me feel better. It doesn't work. And trying to make it seem like you have something similar doesn't work either. Because you very likely don't. If you actually are learning disabled or otherwise neurodiverse, fine! But most people aren't. And I've found that the neurodiverse are less likely to use terms like "differently abled." Many years ago I had a friend who couldn't hear. She said "I'm deaf. Euphemisms are for the differently brained."

You may think that using a term like "differently abled" decreases stigma. It does not. If anything, it increases it. We don't lose stigma by pretending a condition doesn't exist. We lose stigma by recognizing the condition, proclaiming it. That's why my website is called IAmLearningDisabled.com . That's why my first book is called Screwed up Somehow but not Stupid: Life with a Learning Disability. So, what to do instead?

Well, that varies. It depends on what you want to do. If you want to acknowledge me and validate me, call me Peter, but say that I am learning disabled, when that is relevant. If you want to express sympathy, well, sometimes, expressing sympathy means acknowledging that something bad is going on. I use the phrase "that must suck" to stand for what I am talking about, even if I wouldn't use those exact words

If a friend seems upset and you ask what is wrong and they say "my mom just died" you don't say "my mom died too!" and you don't say "that's not so bad! You know Bob? His mom and dad BOTH died!" and you don't say "everyone dies". You say (usually not in these words) 'That must suck."

The other thing you can do is to ask how you can help.

Some people seem to think that if they react this way to someone who is disabled, they are saying "you suck" or something like that. Nonsense! "Disabled" describes me. It does not define me. Yes, I am learning disabled. I'm also a father, a man, retired, curly-haired, divorced, overweight and many other things. Some good, some bad, some neither.

Appendix E

Mainstream

The mainstream is enticing for parents, children, administrators, and politicians, each for their own reasons.

It lets parents imagine that maybe our children aren't so different, so unusual. Maybe they are "normal". Maybe they belong in the mainstream. But maybe not. Maybe our goal ought not be a mainstream education but a mainstream life. After all, your kids will spend about 12 years in elementary and high school, and, if they live to be 80, they will spend about 62 years in our post-high school life.

It also lets kids imagine that they are normal. But the motivations behind that desire are different. Kids don't want to be different. They don't want to take "the short bus". They want to fit in. But I think many kids would embrace special education more readily if the whole notion was not so stigmatized. Kids are less concerned than parents about the future and more concerned about now.

For administrators, mainstreaming is less hassle. And it lets them easily satisfy the requirement of a "least restrictive environment." [1] But we should remember the second part of that phrase "to the maximum extent appropriate". The law was passed to pre-

---

[1] the actual law says limits this by saying "to the maximum extent appropriate" but this limit does not get quoted as often.

vent kids from being shunted to institution-like settings where they would get minimal care and attention.

For bureaucrats, it's cheaper. A lot cheaper. "Least restrictive environment" is also "least expensive environment".

But the mainstream is where some kids drown. I know I would have drowned in the mainstream as an elementary school student, and nearly drowned in the mainstream for junior high school and high school.

And, while the intent is often to mainstream the children and provide extra help to both them and their teachers, too often the help is removed, due to budget cuts or whatever, leaving the kids and the teachers to struggle along. And teachers have hard enough jobs as it is.

Some fish can swim in the mainstream; but some can't.

Appendix F

Lazy

"Lazy, crazy, or stupid" has become a sort of catch-phrase among LDers. There is also a book about ADHD titled *You Mean I'm not Stupid, Lazy, or Crazy?*

I've been called lazy a whole lot in my life, almost always by teachers who had no clue. Sometimes they used the euphemism "does not apply himself". The best teacher who ever taught me, on the other hand, said I tried harder than almost anyone.

"Lazy" is a four letter word. It should never be used in front of children. Nor about children. Because there is no way for a teacher (or anyone but the kid, really) to know how hard the kid is trying, or even what they are trying at. A child with a disability is constantly trying to overcome or get around or just deal with the disability. And no one else can know what that is like for the individual.

One important aspect of being LD in general and being NLD in particular is that things that NT people do without effort take effort from us. You won't see it. It's not like a person on crutches who you can see working hard to ambulate. But the effort is there all the same. It's draining. And it leaves us less effort to spend on homework.

This can also sometimes explain why a kid who is well-behaved all day at school has frequent meltdowns at home. She's exhausted! And every behaves worse when they are exhausted.

Appendix G

Hey!

Hey! World! If someone tells you they are disabled, listen to them! And don't deny it and don't minimize it and don't tell them that you have that too, unless you really, really do. I know you want to help. I know you're trying to be nice. But sometimes, all you can do is say "Wow. That must suck!" And ask what you can do to help. People don't fake having learning disabilities. They fake *not* having them.

Appendix H

Acknowledgements

For the actual writing of the book, I owe a huge debt to Nelsie Spencer and all the members of her Round Table and to Kelly Caldwell and all my classmates in various Memoir classes at Gotham Writers' Workshop.

Printed in the USA
CPSIA information can be obtained
at www.ICGtesting.com
LVHW011205040624
782220LV00001B/16